Contemporary Issues
in Mediation

Volume 4

Related Titles by the Author

Contemporary Issues in Mediation Volume 1
ISBN: 978-981-3108-35-6
ISBN: 978-981-3108-36-3 (pbk)

Contemporary Issues in Mediation Volume 2
ISBN: 978-981-3225-63-3
ISBN: 978-981-3225-64-0 (pbk)

Contemporary Issues in Mediation Volume 3
ISBN: 978-981-3270-81-7
ISBN: 978-981-3271-76-0 (pbk)

Contemporary Issues in Mediation

Volume 4

Joel Lee & Marcus Lim
with Agnes Lo
Singapore International Mediation Institute, Singapore

Guest Editor: Lum Kit-Wye

Published by

World Scientific Publishing Co. Pte. Ltd.

5 Toh Tuck Link, Singapore 596224

USA office: 27 Warren Street, Suite 401-402, Hackensack, NJ 07601

UK office: 57 Shelton Street, Covent Garden, London WC2H 9HE

Library of Congress Cataloging-in-Publication Data
Names: Lee, Joel, editor. | Lim, Marcus, editor.
Title: Contemporary issues in mediation (v. 1) / Edited by Joel Lee
    (Singapore International Mediation Institute, Singapore),
    Marcus Lim (Singapore International Mediation Institute, Singapore).
Description: Hackensack, New Jersey : World Scientific, 2016.
Identifiers: LCCN 2016004240| ISBN 9789813108356 (hardcover : alk. paper) |
    ISBN 9789813108363 (pbk.)
Subjects: LCSH: Dispute resolution (Law) | Mediation. | Dispute resolution (Law)--Singapore. |
Mediation--Singapore.
Classification: LCC K2390 .C667 2016 | DDC 347/.09--dc23
LC record available at http://lccn.loc.gov/2016004240

Contemporary issues in mediation (v. 4)
ISBN 978-981-120-911-6
ISBN 978-981-120-928-4 (pbk)

British Library Cataloguing-in-Publication Data
A catalogue record for this book is available from the British Library.

Copyright © 2020 by World Scientific Publishing Co. Pte. Ltd.

All rights reserved. This book, or parts thereof, may not be reproduced in any form or by any means, electronic or mechanical, including photocopying, recording or any information storage and retrieval system now known or to be invented, without written permission from the publisher.

For photocopying of material in this volume, please pay a copying fee through the Copyright Clearance Center, Inc., 222 Rosewood Drive, Danvers, MA 01923, USA. In this case permission to photocopy is not required from the publisher.

For any available supplementary material, please visit
https://www.worldscientific.com/worldscibooks/10.1142/11521#t=suppl

Typeset by Stallion Press
Email: enquiries@stallionpress.com

Contents

Foreword for the Series		vii
By William Ury		
About the Guest Editor		xi
About the Editors		xiii
Editors' Note		xv
About the CIIM Essay Competition		xix

Part 1 Getting to and Beyond Mediation   **1**

1. What's in a Nudge? How Choice Architecture Surrounding Dispute Resolution Options Can Increase Uptake of Mediation   3
   Charmaine Yap Yun Ning

2. Mediation, Legal Education and the Adversarial Culture in Singapore   15
   Lim Wei Yang

3. A Comparative Guide to Drafting Enforceable Mediation Clauses   25
   Maryam Salehijam

4. Enforcing Mediation Settlement Agreements: An Examination of the Draft Convention on International Settlement Agreements Resulting from Mediation   33
   Chia Chen Wei

vi *Contemporary Issues in Mediation Volume 4*

Part 2 Mediation Obligations and Ethics 43

5. Mediator Neutrality in Singapore: The Siren Call for a
   Paradigm Shift 45
   Kuek Kai Liang

6. The Case for Confidentiality: Singapore's Mediation Act 55
   Nadene Law Qin Ning

7. A Review of Mediator Neutrality 67
   Ivan Ng Yi Fan

8. The Ethical Boundaries of Honesty in Mediation 75
   Lew Zi Qi

Part 3 Mediation Skills 85

9. Negotiating with Children and How that Teaches Us to Be
   Better Mediators 87
   Ho Ting En

10. Learning from Crises: How Crisis Negotiation Skills
    Can Help Mediators Deal with Parties in Mediation 97
    Ang Wen Qi Therese

11. Equal but Different? Exploring How Gender Roles
    Shape the Power Balance in Family-Related Mediation 109
    Lee Kwang Chian

12. Are All Expressions of Anger Equal or Are Some More
    Equal Than Others? 119
    Wesley Aw Ming Xuan

End Notes 127

Foreword for the Series

By William Ury

A young man was hiking through the woods. He came to a clearing and sat on a rock to rest. As he ate his lunch, he noticed an old man moving through the clearing in a very deliberate way. The man would walk a specific number of steps, poke a hole in the ground with his walking stick, drop something in and then repeat the process. Curious, the young man approached the old man and asked him what he was doing.

The old man replied, "Well, I'm planting trees."
"But why?" the young man asked.
"When I was younger," the old man said, "this entire land was filled with trees. But over time, many trees had been cut down. I come here every day to plant trees."
Fascinated, the young man asked, "How long have you been doing this?"
"Forty years." was the matter of fact reply.
"Forty years!" exclaimed the young man.
"Yup," the old man replied. Gesturing to a grove of young trees in the distance, he said with some pride, "I planted those 10 years ago." The young man was incredulous. "That's great but these trees will take a long time to grow! And, if you will pardon me saying so, you may not live long enough to see the seeds you are planting today grow into trees!"

> *"This is true," said the old man "I have lived long enough to see some of the fruits of my labour. But the seeds I plant today are not for me, but for you."*

It has now been just about 40 years since I had the privilege of embarking on the adventure of teaching and practicing in the field of negotiation and mediation. During that time, I have had the joy of learning from and working with many highly talented and skilled individuals in academia, law, business and diplomacy. In those early days, there was very little scholarly writing in this area. After all, the field was relatively new and viewed by many with caution, if not outright skepticism.

Over the years, I have been gratified to watch the field of mediation grow considerably. Today, practitioners, teachers and researchers can be found in every part of the world. The teaching, practice and scholarship of negotiation and mediation constitute a dynamic system in which each contributes to the others. New tools and frameworks have been developed as a result of research, taught to practitioners, and then tested and refined in the field, which in turn has informed further research. This interplay between theory and practice has been vital in developing new insights and methods.

Yet the field of negotiation and mediation is still young. As we look back on the progress, we might be satisfied with the seeds we have planted which have sprouted into trees. Yet, as the concepts and practices spread around the world, we have a responsibility to ensure that future generations will be able to build on all that has been achieved. We must continue to plant seeds, not for ourselves, but for those to come.

This is why this book project by the Singapore International Mediation Institute is such a timely endeavour worthy of support. It is said that a journey of a thousand miles begins with a single step. The Singapore International Mediation Institute is taking that first step to inspire the youth of today and encourage them to engage in scholarship about mediation. It provides them the platform and the opportunity to plant seeds for the benefit and enjoyment of future generations.

As the first of its kind in Singapore, I look forward to seeing this book series not only continue to flourish, but also to show the way forward through innovative and thought-provoking work.

And I take this opportunity to wish you much success in getting to yes!

William Ury
Co-founder, Harvard Negotiation Project
Co-author, *Getting to Yes*
31 May 2016

About the Guest Editor

Lum Kit-Wye is an Associate Professor and the Associate Dean (Undergraduate Student Life) at the Nanyang Business School, Nanyang Technological University (NTU) where she teaches business law, negotiation and dispute resolution to both the undergraduates and the participants of the Nanyang MBA. Kit-Wye obtained her Bachelor of Laws and Master of Laws from the Faculty of Law, National University of Singapore. Kit-Wye is on the Singapore International Mediation Centre's panel of International Mediators, a Principal Mediator with the Singapore Mediation Centre, an accredited mediator on the Panel of Mediators with the State Courts Centre for Dispute Resolution, a SIMI Certified Mediator and an IMI Certified Mediator.

Kit-Wye is an experienced trainer and has conducted many negotiation and conflict resolution workshops for members of judiciaries, government agencies and private organisations in Singapore, Brunei, the Philippines, Cambodia, Fiji, India, Sri Lanka and Thailand.

In 2002, Kit-Wye was awarded NTU's Teacher of the Year Award for the Nanyang Business School. Kit-Wye also received the Nanyang Business School Award for Teacher of the Division in 2002. In 2012, Kit-Wye received the Nanyang Business School Divisional Teaching Excellence Award. In 2015, she was given the Outstanding Volunteer Award in recognition of her contribution as a volunteer mediator at the Singapore State Courts.

About the Editors

Joel Lee

Joel Lee is the Chairman of the Singapore International Mediation Institute (SIMI) and a Professor at the Faculty of Law, National University of Singapore. Joel co-pioneered the teaching of negotiation and mediation at the tertiary level in Singapore and has played a significant role in furthering the development of mediation in Singapore, not just in education but in practice. A graduate of Victoria University of Wellington and Harvard Law School, Joel is an affiliate partner with CMPartners (USA), and a principal mediator with and the Training Director of the Singapore Mediation Centre (SMC).

Joel is an adjudicator with the Financial Industry Disputes Resolution Centre and was a member of the International Mediation Institute's Independent Standards Commission and Intercultural Taskforce. He was also a key member of the Ministry of Law's Working Group on International Commercial Mediation. Joel is currently the founding Chairman of the Board of Directors at SIMI.

Joel has taught overseas at the University of Copenhagen (Denmark), University of Law, Economics and Science of Aix-Marseille (Aix-en-Provence France) and Anglia Law School (UK), and is the co-editor and co-author of the book *An Asian Perspective on Mediation* and the General Editor for the *Asian Journal on Mediation*. In 2011, Joel was awarded the Outstanding Educator Award which is the National University of Singapore's highest teaching award.

Marcus Lim

Marcus Lim is the Executive Director of SIMI. He is also a part-time Lecturer for the Negotiation and Mediation Workshops at the Faculty of Law, National University of Singapore, and was the co-ordinator for both courses in 2017. A graduate from the prestigious Law and Business Double Degree programme of the National University of Singapore, he is also a consultant with CMPartners (USA).

In the mediation field, Marcus is an Associate Mediator with the Singapore Mediation Centre, a court-appointed volunteer mediator for the Small Claims Tribunal at the State Courts, as well as member of the Healthcare Mediator Panel under the MOHH Healthcare Mediation Scheme. Prior to joining SIMI, Marcus practiced at Rajah & Tann LLP's Competition and Technology, Media and Telecommunications Practice Group.

Marcus has extensive experience conducting negotiation and mediation trainings for staff and management of government organisations, as well as multinational corporations across many sectors, such as financial, retail, real estate, IT, education and the healthcare industry.

Editors' Note

It has been four years since the first volume of Contemporary Issues In Mediation and the book has not only seen a growing pool of contributors, but a growing diversity and depth in the issues covered. This volume is special as it coincides with the signing of the Singapore Convention on Mediation in Singapore to make it easier for businesses to enforce mediated settlement agreements.

The journey through Volumes 1 to 3 has seen an increase in submissions from the two law schools in Singapore and beyond, and a strong interest in areas such as the evolving mediation landscape, mediation and social justice and mediation skills, which were the focus for Volume 3.

Expanding on Volume 3, Volume 4 is dedicated to three categories: getting to and beyond mediation, mediation obligations and ethics, and mediation skills. The contributors for Volume 4 included a submission from a JD student from the Singapore Management University and a PhD student from the University of Ghent, Belgium. This signifies a growing interest in mediation across different student profiles and a sign of the increasing reach of the series on mediation students locally and internationally.

In Part 1, Getting to and Beyond Mediation, we have the top entry by Charmaine Yap on how the use of nudges and choice architecture can increase uptake of mediation vis-à-vis other dispute resolution methods. Celebrating the signing of the Singapore Convention on Mediation, Maryam Salehijam provides some guidance on how to draft enforceable mediation clauses, while Chia Chen Wei analyses the draft Convention on international settlement agreements resulting from mediation and its potential impact on both international and local mediation practice. Lim Wei Yang offers his insights on expanding the role of the National University of Singapore's Faculty of Law in the promotion of mediation in the Singapore legal system, for more holistic and collaborative dispute resolution.

In Part 2, Mediation Obligations and Ethics, first runner up, Kuek Kai Liang calls for a paradigm shift in mediator neutrality towards a more nuanced and contextual approach to mediation ethics in Singapore, which juxtaposes Ivan Ng's review of mediator neutrality and how it interacts with self-determination or justice. Nadene Law discusses the case for confidentiality in the Singapore's newly enacted Mediation Act, while Lew Zi Qi explores the boundaries of the mediation advocate's ethical duties of honesty in mediation.

In Part 3, Mediation Skills, Ho Ting En introduces the idea of negotiating with children to become better mediators, while Therese Ang explores how crisis negotiation skills can help mediators to better deal with emotion or difficult parties to facilitate dispute resolution. Lee Kwang Chian explores how gender roles shape the power balance in family-related mediation and ending Part 3 with a bang, Wesley Aw studies the different expressions of anger to help mediators decide when and whether to elicit emotions during a mediation.

As always, this publication would not have been possible without the support and efforts of many people. We would like to take this opportunity to express our heartfelt thanks to:

- Our amazing better halves, Pearl, Li Jing and Mark, for their unending patience and love;
- Mr William Ury, for writing the foreword for the series;
- Members of SIMI's board, past and present, for their unwavering support of the project (Mr Poon Hong Yuen, Mr Han Kok Juan, Professor Nadja Alexander, Ms Josephine Hadikusumo, Mr Michael Leathes and Ms Irena Vanenkova);
- The Singapore Ministry of Law, for continuing to support our work;
- The National University of Singapore, Faculty of Law, for their invaluable assistance for our operations;

- Our publishers, the World Scientific Publishing Company, for their patience and guidance in bringing another volume to publication; and
- Our students (past and present) from the National University of Singapore, Faculty of Law, and Nanyang Business School at the Nanyang Technological University, as well as all over the world, for always being an inspiration to our work.

Last but not least, we would like to thank you, the reader, for supporting SIMI and this book. We hope that this project continues to inspire you in your work, whatever field it may be, to find collaborative solutions in resolving your disputes.

Joel Lee, Marcus Lim and Lum Kit-Wye
Singapore
5 August 2019

About the CIIM Essay Competition

As part of SIMI's (Singapore International Mediation Institute) mission to promote awareness and interest in mediation, SIMI regularly organises an essay competition to help promote mediation academia among undergraduates and students in tertiary institutions. Submissions are welcome from students not only pursuing studies in law but also other disciplines. Selected entries will be featured in an annual edition of the *Contemporary Issues in Mediation*, with attractive prizes for some of the best submissions.

About SIMI

The Singapore International Mediation Institute (SIMI) was incorporated on 15 July 2014 as a non-profit organisation supported by the Ministry of Law. SIMI is a subsidiary of the National University of Singapore (NUS) and is housed at the NUS Faculty of Law.

SIMI is headed by an international Board of Directors with representatives from both mediation practitioners as well as corporate users of mediation, to further its mission to (1) set and achieve high mediation standards through the professionalisation of mediation; (2) promote understanding and inspire the use of mediation; (3) stimulate and facilitate the development and growth of mediation through research and innovation; and (4) foster a strong mediation community in Asia by engaging stakeholders in discussion, events and outreach activities.

Getting to and Beyond Mediation

What's in a Nudge? How Choice Architecture Surrounding Dispute Resolution Options Can Increase Uptake of Mediation

Charmaine Yap Yun Ning

I. Introduction

The steadily growing prominence of mediation in Singapore's dispute resolution landscape belies the two decades-long journey in getting the legal profession, businesses and the public to embrace mediation.[1] For mediation proponents, it may seem an agonisingly protracted process given mediation's oft-cited benefits and suitability for many disputes.

A behavioural economist may attribute disputants' failure to choose mediation to cognitive errors and motivational distortions. Under the Rational Choice Theory, we might expect greater uptake of a dispute resolution method that is generally cheaper, faster and preserves relationships. A utility-maximising *homo economicus* would rationally conclude that mediation would lead to an outcome that has higher utility than litigation.

However, well-known behavioural experiments have shown that the cognitive limitations and mental short-cuts used in decision-making may lead to decisions that seem irrational under the Rational Choice Theory. This may explain the continuing under-utilisation of mediation in many areas despite being so lauded.

In 2017, 538 matters were filed with the Singapore Mediation Centre.[2] This number is dwarfed by the total of 57,237 civil cases filed with the State Courts and the Supreme Court in the same year. A 2016 study by the Singapore Academy of Law found that only 5% of respondents involved in cross-border transactions preferred mediation as a dispute resolution method.[3]

Understanding our underlying mental processes will lead to better predictions of how we actually respond to rules and help in formulating measures that are more effective in encouraging mediation.[4] As we are irrational in predictable ways, behavioural economists make the case for structuring the context surrounding choices and using nudges to influence people to make better decisions. This is known as choice architecture.[5] Choice architecture is inevitable as the option to mediate will necessarily be framed within a context that will influence the decision-making.[6]

Nudges and its underlying regulatory philosophy of libertarian paternalism is uniquely suited for mediation. While family mediations and certain government and industry-specific mediations have been made mandatory, this approach may be unsuitable for most private domestic and international mediations where there are less compelling reasons for undercutting party autonomy. Nudges preserve freedom of choice which is more consistent with the core mediation principles of consent and autonomy.

Rather than leaving it to unintentional or uninformed design, it will be argued that we should ethically and thoughtfully design choices to nudge disputants towards mediation. Governments, mediation service providers, mediation accreditation institutes, mediators, mediation advocates and academics are all potential choice architects.[7] This chapter will explore the cognitive tendencies that explain the under-utilisation of mediation, analyse existing measures based on behavioural economics insights, and make proposals for refining current approaches and for new measures.

II. Behavioural economics explanations: Why parties do not mediate as much as they should

A. *Cognitive biases*

(1) *Status quo bias*

Behavioural findings suggest that individuals prefer the status quo and will tend to stick with a default option. Three explanations have been proffered to explain this — inertia, endorsement and loss aversion.

Deciding against a default rule involves an active effort to focus on the problem, form a preference and reject that rule. Given the power of inertia, many would continue with the status quo. This is especially where the question is a complex one entailing more mental effort.[8] Determining which dispute resolution method would leave one better off involves weighing difficult trade-offs between time costs, financial costs, probabilities of legal success and emotional costs. Disputants might choose to avoid this altogether by going with the default option.

Parties may also perceive the default rule as an implicit endorsement of that option by the choice architects. People may believe that the default was chosen for good reason and would defer to what has been chosen for them unless they have private information that justifies a change.[9] There is a situation of significant information asymmetry for first-time or one-off disputants who lack experience when faced with intimidating court processes.

Finally, the default rule establishes a reference point. Costs incurred in deviating from the default rule are construed as a loss. Behavioural studies have found that people are loss averse — they dislike losses far more than corresponding gains. Individuals may thus prefer to stick with a default rule to avoid a loss which may take the form of time costs, financial costs and emotional costs such as regret.[10]

In dispute resolution, litigation or arbitration tends to be seen as the status quo. The status quo bias means that even when provided with perfect information on a better alternative, people tend to select the default. Where parties are less familiar with mediation processes, they would prefer to continue with litigation or arbitration even if mediation is the rationally better choice.

(2) *Overconfidence bias*

A bias that will come as no surprise to those involved in dispute resolution is the tendency for people to be unrealistically optimistic when predicting their behaviour and prospects. This systematic bias occurs even when the individual is factually informed.[11]

Academic literature has sought to explain bargaining impasses because of unrealistic optimism affecting both parties. In negotiations, this self-serving bias leads parties to believe they deserve more and impedes settlement.[12] Not only does the bias affect behaviour during bargaining, it influences parties' choices on dispute resolution methods.

Disputants may choose litigation because of an inflated view of their chances of success.

One reason offered for this bias is asymmetry in how people process information. Individuals are more likely to change their beliefs when given good news, whilst their views are more likely to stay the same when the news is bad.[13]

The implication of this behavioural finding is that merely providing statistical information that mediation is better than adjudication in a general sense may be defeated by parties' unrealistic optimism. Measures taken would instead need to go further and persuade parties that mediation is better than litigation in their augmented perception.[14]

(3) *Salience bias*

Some aspects of decision-making are vivid and perceptible while others are diffused, shrouded and difficult to quantify. Our limited attention span and imperfect information cause a bias in our behaviour towards what is most salient. There may be attributes that are important but do not receive sufficient consideration because they are not salient and do not catch our attention.[15]

One form of salience is the visibility of litigation over mediation in the media. Simply by dint of media exposure, parties feel more familiar with the litigation process.[16]

Another shrouded but important attribute is long-term costs and benefits. This leads to present bias where individuals pay too much attention to the short-term and apply very high discount rates to future costs and benefits.[17] At the beginning of a dispute, parties might be more preoccupied with defending their legal rights and underestimate the financial and emotional costs of doing so.

Our limited attention span and inability to apply appropriate temporal discount rates means that the simple provision of information may not be enough to produce optimal behaviour. Information should be presented in a way that ensures salient attributes are made known to the individual. Complexity and information overload may lead to important features being missed.[18]

B. *Inability to accurately predict utility*

While we might assume individuals to be the best judge of their own utility, research has shown that people have difficulties predicting their own experience. Mapping is the ability to predict the relationship between a choice and the ultimate utility derived from that decision. Individuals are not able to accurately map and select options that will make them better off especially if the decision is complex.

Comparing dispute resolution processes involves weighing time costs, financial costs, probabilities of legal success and emotional costs. These complex trade-offs will not be immediately evident to disputants unless they are repeat players.[19] Efforts to educate the objective benefits of the various dispute resolution methods cannot replicate stakes, emotions and pressure involved in real adjudication.

C. *Focus on appearance of fairness*

Classical economics presumes that individuals are self-interested. However, experiments suggest that people want to be seen to act fairly and will not violate norms of fairness even when it is in their economic interest to do so.

On the flip side, when an individual perceives something to be unfair to themselves they may choose to defend their interests through litigation even when doing so is not in their self-interest. Self-serving bias further complicates things as our notion of fairness may be biased in favour of ourselves. When parties have different self-interested notions of fairness, they interpret behaviours by the other party not as an attempt to get what they perceive as fair but as an attempt to gain an unfair advantage.[20]

Under a narrow, rights-based conception, fairness may seem to require vindication of legal rights. In his 2017 keynote address at the Law Society Mediation Forum, Chief Justice Sundaresh Menon talked about the need to move away from this restricted conception of Rule of Law based on legal rights.[21] However, some may nevertheless persist with the view that the informality and interest-based approach of mediation does not accord fairness in the context of legal rights and responsibilities.[22]

III. Applying behavioural economics insights to practice: Evaluating existing measures and proposing reforms

A. *Presumption of ADR in setting a default rule*

The Presumption of Alternative Dispute Resolution (ADR) for all civil cases under the State Courts Practice Directions[23] creates a default rule. The Court will automatically refer all cases to the most appropriate mode of ADR unless parties opt out.[24] Parties and solicitors must fill out an ADR form to facilitate the decision on the ADR options and any party who wishes to opt out must indicate her/his decision in the ADR form.[25]

This increases the likelihood that parties will simply end up in the mediation process by operation of the status quo bias. Parties who want to opt out of mediation must justify their decision in the ADR form and to the court. This imposes additional time and effort costs which individuals prone to inertia will be disinclined to incur.

The Presumption of ADR is also a clear normative statement by the government and courts that interest-based dispute resolution is more desirable for individuals. This suggests to disputants that mediation is a norm endorsed by society, tapping into our desire to conform with societal norms.

Finally, making ADR the default frames the decision not to mediate as a loss which might come with cognitive and emotional cost such as regret, using individuals' loss aversion to great effect.

(1) *Presentation of information about mediation in facilitating choice mapping*

Public education to change behaviours cannot merely involve the simple provision of information given our cognitive biases and failings. Information provision will only be meaningful in affecting decisions made if it helps parties map choices onto their expected utility accurately. This is especially important where the choice is a complex one.

Solicitors now have a professional duty to advise clients about ADR under the Supreme Court Practice Directions. This is one way information about mediation can be provided. Further, the Legal Profession

Professional Conduct Rules require a solicitor to evaluate the use of ADR processes in an appropriate case.[26]

One method to help people better map utility onto choices is to present information in practical rather than technical terms that actually means something to the individual.[27] The ADR form under the State Court Practice Directions provide users with information about ADR processes to guide their decisions.[28] Appendix I of the Supreme Court Practice Directions also provides guidelines for lawyers advising about ADR.[29] The ADR form and Appendix I do go some way in presenting information meaningfully by highlighting practical considerations and examples of likely outcomes in easy-to-understand terms.

A further proposal might be to include "before and after" scenarios which help users make the comparison between "how you are feeling right now" and "how people using mediation emerge after".[30] This helps to address the difficulty disputants face in predicting the utility that they will derive from mediation. More specific comparators may also help disputants' decision-making.[31] For instance, the average timeframes, the costs involved or success rates for the various dispute resolution methods could be provided in the same document.

Another method for helping people cope with complex decisions is to structure choices. For simple decisions, the individual can do a cost-benefit analysis of the alternatives available. When faced with complex decisions, people employ simplifying strategies such as elimination by aspects or collaborative filtering.[32] A study found that as decisions became more complex, people were more likely to use an elimination strategy but the percentage of information considered decreased.[33] This may have the effect of less-than-optimal decisions being made. A choice architect can help people make better choices by providing a structure for decision-making.

The ADR form does this by distilling key attributes of ADR processes into a mindmap. Appendix I achieves a similar effect by providing a table which highlights key points of comparison between litigation and mediation and addressing issues such as confidentiality, length, cost, relationship and emotions. This simplifies the cost-benefit analysis for parties choosing between the various ADR methods.

(2) *Providing opportunities to adopt mediation at multiple points in dispute resolution process*

Well-designed systems expect human error and are forgiving of mistakes.[34] The opportunity to adopt ADR at multiple points of the dispute resolution process allows parties to subsequently change course when the costs of litigation become more evident. This recognises that parties may not be able to accurately evaluate the costs of adjudication until they have experienced some of the time, financial and relational costs for themselves.

One strategy for addressing human error is to use checklists which help with memory recall by increasing the salience of certain information.[35] A similar effect is achieved by the notification sent out by Singapore Mediation Centre (SMC) on the option of mediation at the end of pleadings and around the date of the Pre-Trial Conference (PTC). This increases the salience of mediation as a dispute resolution method at a key point in the litigation process, allowing parties to elect for an alternative method of dispute resolution.

A proposal for increasing the notification's effectiveness is to time the reminder when the information would be most salient to parties. After pleadings and around the date of the PTC, parties may still be too raw from the dispute or hot for a fight. Further, overconfidence and confirmation bias would be operating strongly having just made their arguments in the pleadings which would reinforce perceptions of the strength of their case.

Stages of proceedings where reminders may be more effective are at the stage of specific discovery or at the doorstep of trial. After discovery, parties are confronted with the available evidence which may serve to mitigate their overconfidence. The commencement of trial is where parties would be faced with exponentially escalating legal fees. The factor of financial costs would be brought into sharper focus for parties and mediation may become a more cost-effective option. Further, the prospect of giving evidence and being cross-examined on the stand highlights the pressures and emotional costs of the litigation process, making the relationship-preserving nature of mediation more attractive.

(3) *Relooking the label of "alternative dispute resolution"*

The suggestion to replace the terminology of "alternative dispute resolution" with "appropriate dispute resolution" is not merely a cosmetic or principled change. It changes the frame through which we view mediation.

Labelling mediation as an "alternative" implicitly suggests that litigation is the primary and default mode of dispute resolution. Our status quo bias would operate to favour litigation as the norm. Mediation and other forms of ADR might be seen as being inferior or reflecting a compromise compared to the norm.[36]

Chief Justice Sundaresh Menon has highlighted the need for a paradigm shift away from seeing ADR as alternative to traditional court systems to an essential element in toolkit available to resolve disputes.[37] He noted that this shift has occurred with the reforms to the Family Justice Courts where mediation, counselling and other ADR measures are necessary, not alternative, elements to the court process.[38] Outside of the family context where mandatory mediation might not be as desirable, a change in terminology might help to lead a shift in practice towards seeing mediation as a dispute resolution method in its own right.

(4) *Framing choices through fee schedules*

Offering disputants fewer but well-framed choices might be an effective and targeted nudge towards mediation. While there has been a proliferation of ADR methods including mediation, neutral evaluation, arbitration and litigation, studies have found that choosers faced with too many alternatives can experience choice overload where they are inclined not to choose or to surrender the choice to someone.[39]

Alexander (2014) suggests cutting down on the number of ADR processes that are offered to disputants and proposes that dispute resolution service providers might frame the options in fee schedule in the following way:

1. Arbitration: $10,000 per arbitrator per day;
2. Mediation: $10,000 per mediator per day;
3. Arbitration and mediation: $10,000 per mediator/arbitrator per day.[40]

In a behavioural study adopting a similar formula, the presence of the second option significantly increased the number of people who chose the third option as compared to where only options one and three were available.[41] A similar formula could be adopted by Singapore International Mediation Centre (SIMC) and Singapore International Arbitration Centre (SIAC) in their fee schedules to increase uptake of the Arb-Med-Arb Protocol (AMA Protocol).

(5) *Adopting opt-out rules for mediation in arbitration processes*

One proposal that leverages on the status quo bias is to make mediation an opt-out procedure in international commercial arbitrations. The benefits of embedding mediation within arbitration is that users familiar with arbitration are introduced to a relatively new procedure within familiar terrain.[42] Under most arbitration rules, mediation is currently an opt-in process where parties can choose to incorporate mediation.[43]

The findings of a 2013 survey by the International Mediation Institute suggest that parties want an intermediate between mandatory mediation and active encouragement to mediate.[44] The American Arbitration Association's ("AAA") amended "Commercial Arbitration Rules and Mediation Procedures" published in 2013 provides such an intermediate by mandating mediation unless parties opt out.[45]

The approach the SIAC and SIMC has taken in marrying international commercial arbitration and mediation is through the AMA Protocol. It remains an opt-in process to the extent that parties must incorporate the Singapore AMA clause into their contracts or agree to submit their dispute for resolution under the AMA Protocol. As of 2017, nine cases have been filed under the AMA Protocol since it was introduced in November 2014.[46] It remains to be seen whether more parties can be encouraged to incorporate the AMA clause or to submit their disputes to the AMA Protocol. Should a stronger nudge towards mediation be required, the opt-out approach of the AAA is a potential model for consideration.

IV. Conclusion

This chapter has sought to provide a preliminary behavioural economics account of why parties do not mediate as often as one would rationally expect. Understanding the underlying mental processes that drive human behaviour helps in designing informed and intentional choice architecture surrounding mediation that can nudge disputants towards better decisions.

There is scope for more research into applying behavioural economics to improve decision-making surrounding dispute resolution methods. The proposals provided are based on behavioural studies conducted in other areas such as consumer behaviour and health in a Western context. Further empirical studies could be conducted on decision-making of Singapore court users in dispute resolution to determine whether these observations hold true for choice architecture surrounding mediation in the local context. Another worthwhile area of study could be the behavioural motivations of counsel who advise clients on mediation and what nudges can be applied to them.

While terms such as "cognitive failures or errors" and "motivational distortions" that are commonly used in this field of studies have been applied, these cognitive tendencies should not be seen as failures that need to be corrected. Rather they are part and parcel of the human condition that can be harnessed productively by intelligent choice architecture to help us make better decisions. Ultimately, policy-making surrounding mediation would be better served by a fuller view of decision-makers as human beings — with their idiosyncrasies and biases — than as cold and calculated automatons.

Mediation, Legal Education and the Adversarial Culture in Singapore

Lim Wei Yang

Much has been said about developing the mediation scene in Singapore, whether as a centre for international commercial mediation or to increase the uptake of community mediation. The value of mediation today is now undeniable,[1] and to this end, numerous service providers have been established.[2] However, a key stakeholder that has largely remained dormant throughout the transformation in the mediation landscape is the law school, in particular, the National University of Singapore's Faculty of Law ("NUS").[3] Despite being the leading law school in Asia, NUS seems to be flying under the radar in the mediation scene. It does not boast of contributions to developing mediation as much as it trumpets other academic achievements, and plans for the future of mediation make little to no mention of NUS.

This chapter aims to draw attention to the important role that NUS plays in paving the way for mediation to play a bigger role in Singapore's legal system. Lamentably, not only does legal education at NUS not prepare its graduates to resolve disputes through mediation, its compulsory curriculum arguably conditions students to think of litigation as the paradigm dispute resolution tool. As Singapore continues to strengthen its mediation infrastructure, a rethink of the education that students receive at NUS is apposite. While the biggest gains may only result from substantial changes to the curriculum, modest improvements can nevertheless be achieved even if minor adjustments can be made to the current pedagogy. Part I of this chapter highlights several practical reasons why law schools should pay more attention to mediation, Part II explores how the current law school curriculum inadvertently creates a paradigm that is unconducive for mediation and Part III offers several suggestions for improvement. While some of these arguments may apply to other dispute resolution processes like negotiation, this chapter focuses exclusively on mediation.

I. Why NUS should care

Legal education at NUS has come a long way since it was first pioneered by L.A. Sheridan, who believed that it was *not* the faculty's job to produce lawyers competent for practice. To him, NUS was to be concerned with teaching doctrine and reasoning, and not with imparting professional expertise.[4] However, over the years, more efforts have been made to provide students with more practical experience,[5] with an increasing emphasis on problem solving, "lawyering" and helping others.[6] In line with this shift, it is submitted that a greater emphasis on mediation is warranted for several reasons.

A. *Relevance*

Firstly, legal education must keep up with the demands of clients as well as evolving legal practices[7] or risk being left behind. Mediation is slowly but surely growing in popularity as a mode of dispute resolution.[8] While it is unclear whether this increasing popularity is driven by lawyers or their clients, one can expect clients to increasingly prefer mediation as they better appreciate its benefits. This is especially so for commercial clients, who can obtain business-oriented solutions that improve relationships through mediation that litigation cannot provide.[9] Such a change in client preferences will affect the expectations that clients have of their lawyers, in the sense that they are likely be expected to be familiar with their clients' business and commercial objectives.[10] Lawyers must thus realise that winning cases is not the same as winning in business,[11] and that more often than not, clients care more about the latter.

To this end, lawyers must be competent in a range of dispute resolution processes that most suits their clients' interests. Mediation or mediation advocacy is one such important tool that lawyers need to add to their toolbox, or risk being unable to "fully and thoughtfully serve their clients' true interests and needs in the most effective way possible".[12] To the extent that law schools are geared towards preparing their graduates for the legal profession and equipping them to deliver quality legal service,[13] not preparing students for mediation is a missed opportunity to train lawyers who are also commercially astute professionals.[14] As Singapore's legal practices evolve, perhaps it is better for NUS to take the initiative, rather than play catch-up later on.

B. *Wider societal interests*

A second reason why NUS should place greater emphasis on mediation is to promote the wider societal interest that motivates the higher level push for mediation. Mediation is an integral part of Singapore's justice system for both private commercial disputes and community disputes,[15] both of which are promoted for different reasons. The push to make Singapore an international commercial mediation centre is part of its wider goal of strengthening its position as an international dispute resolution centre.[16] The hope is that this will stimulate the market for Singaporean legal services and help to develop domestic legal expertise. This in turn is meant to bolster Singapore's attractiveness as a business hub in order to boost other parts of the economy as well.[17]

On the other hand, community mediation is promoted as the preferred way of resolving relational disputes in a community because of its capability for building neighbourliness, forging a *kampong* spirit, as well as cultivating good relationships and tolerance.[18] In other words, it is the form of dispute resolution that best preserves the social fabric, and shapes a less fractious and more harmonious society.[19] This is particularly important in densely populated Singapore where the inherent possibility of conflict is higher due to the greater degree of interaction between people.[20] As an institution that strives for the betterment of society through service,[21] surely promoting mediation is an opportunity that should not be missed.

C. *Correcting the adversarial culture*

Finally, NUS should pay more attention to mediation because there is an ingrained adversarial culture[22] in Singapore that needs to be corrected.

18   *Contemporary Issues in Mediation Volume 4*

This adversarial culture, which impedes the uptake of mediation, refers to the tendency for lawyers to prefer litigation over other forms of dispute resolution. Even where the lawyer wishes to act differently, he/she is pressured into reciprocating an adversarial approach.[23] However, if the goal is to embed mediation into Singapore's DNA,[24] then this culture cannot be allowed to continue. Lawyers who are part of this culture will inevitably influence how their clients experience other forms of dispute resolution. Given that lawyers often act as the voice of reason for their clients, one can easily see how a litigation-inclined lawyer might influence his/her client to think the same way. Even if other forms of dispute resolution are attempted, such a lawyer may detract from his/her client's ability to reach an appropriate resolution.[25]

On this note, it is submitted that NUS is in a prime position to correct this culture. Unlike correcting the bias of a lawyer, which requires one to identify and dismantle the source of that bias, NUS can control the manner and direction in which students are trained from a blank slate. Studies from abroad have shown that integrating appropriate dispute resolution processes into compulsory law school curriculum has the effect of creating an attitude that favours collaborative problem solving as opposed to an adversarial approach.[26] The effects of legal education on the adversarial culture may not be immediately apparent because fresh graduates may not wield the necessary decision-making power. Instead, one can expect to see a gradual change over time as these ex-students rise to positions of authority. NUS should thus capitalise on its privileged position of being able to shape the law student's professional identity as a lawyer skilled in the full spectrum of dispute resolution processes, instead of merely litigation.[27]

II. Unconducive environment for mediation

If one wishes to talk about the professional identities of a NUS law student, it is suggested that the starting point should be the compulsory curriculum at NUS. Not only is it common to *all* law students at NUS,[28] it lays the foundation for all other legal skills that are picked up in the upper-years. The compulsory classes at NUS may be roughly divided into three categories: (1) substantive law[29] courses, (2) legal skills courses[30] and (3) "fluff" courses.[31] Out of 80 compulsory credits, 56 credits (70%) come from substantive law courses, while legal skills and "fluff" courses account for 12 credits (15%) each. There is no compulsory course that focuses exclusively on mediation, nor is there any meaningful exposure to it. Right off the bat, mediation is off to a losing start.

Concerns about law schools not paying enough attention to mediation are not new.[32] The argument is often made that law schools focus on legal analysis *to the exclusion* of other equally important skills, with the result that the graduate is trained to *think* like a lawyer but has to *learn how to be a lawyer* after earning their degree.[33] However, it is submitted that the bifurcation between "thinking" and "doing" is wrong, because being an *effective* mediator/mediation advocate requires one to *think* like one as well. Sadly, instead of inculcating a mindset of collaborative problem solving, the compulsory curriculum at NUS arguably conditions students to *think* in a manner that is incompatible with mediation in three ways: (i) the thought process cultivated, (ii) the outcomes pursued and (iii) the cumulative effect of the compulsory curriculum.

A. *Process*

At NUS, substantive law classes typically involve a mix of lectures and tutorials. Lectures usually provide an exposition of the relevant doctrines and laws, while tutorials act as a platform to further discuss legal issues arising from those laws using a mix of hypothetical fact scenarios ("hypotheticals") and essay questions. The use of hypotheticals, which are not bad *per se*, has the potential to create biases in the way students approach problems, and both students and educators should be aware of this.

Firstly, hypotheticals train students to filter out facts that are irrelevant to the *substantive legal issue* at hand. Important facts that may shed light on the client's underlying interests are thus often wrongly discarded as red herrings. If not managed properly, this mindset may carry on into practice when one interviews a client. The result is that a lawyer may be focused on distilling the client's problem into a legal issue, which drastically oversimplifies it by stripping away the emotional, relational and communication-related problems that are inextricably intertwined with the client's dispute.[34] Sadly, the things stripped away are the *very things* that need to be resolved if the client wants an enduring solution and an amicable end to the matter (which mediation offers).[35]

The second problem, related to the first, arises from how hypotheticals condition students to spot legal issues in the narrative. While this is an extremely valuable skill that any lawyer worth his/her salt should have, the problem is with *only* identifying legal issues, because then one tends to treat every problem as a legal problem. A misunderstanding between business partners becomes a contractual issue, and loud music coming from a neighbour's house becomes an issue in private nuisance. However, the reality is that a client comes to the lawyer with a problem (with no adjective attached), which only takes on the character of a *legal* problem when the lawyer makes it so. Since legal problems are best resolved through the courts, it would come as no surprise that lawyers who are trained to turn problems into *legal* problems are inherently biased towards litigation.

B. *Outcomes*

The problem with hypotheticals extends from the process to the outcomes. In a hypothetical, students are typically asked to advise clients on their rights, and/or whether their claim can succeed in court. Take for example this question in the Torts paper of Academic Year 2014/2015: "Advise Edwin and Katie on all their possible causes of action in tort and who they should sue".[36] The implicit assumption in these scenarios is that the matter will be heard in court, which in turn gives the impression to young law students that every client's problem is likely to head in the same direction, priming him/her to play the role of a "rights warrior" instead of a "conflict resolver" or "peacemaker".[37] Instead of thinking about the problem holistically, the law student thinks about what they can get in court.

The consequence of focusing on the outcomes of litigation is that students are primed to accept the false dichotomy of win-lose thinking when it comes to dispute resolution. That is, the hypothetical client wins if he enforces his rights, and loses if he cannot. Not only is this premise false,[38] it is further entrenched when tutors motivate and encourage their students to try as hard as possible to find a way for the client to "win", such as by suggesting different heads of claim.[39] This leaves little room to cultivate and develop a collaborative approach to dispute resolution that mediation requires.[40]

C. *Cumulative effects*

Hypotheticals aside, two aspects of NUS' compulsory curriculum as a whole contribute towards presenting a distorted view of the duty of lawyers and their requisite skills. First, the bulk of compulsory courses (amounting to 80% of compulsory courses), including the Legal Analysis, Research and Communication course, focusses on analysing the law and arguing about what it should be, which contributes to the adversarial, win-lose mindset detailed earlier. Second, there are no compulsory courses dedicated to collaborative dispute resolution processes, nor do they explore them in depth.[41] Although the Corporate Deals[42] course provides some rudimentary training in negotiation, only half the cohort of second-year students take this course, with the remaining students taking the Trial Advocacy course. This means that while half the cohort receives *basic* training, the other half has the litigation paradigm reinforced.

Looking beyond the compulsory curriculum, courses in collaborative dispute resolution are offered to a very small group of students. The mediation elective at NUS is only run once per year and does not take more than 30 students,[43] which means that, even upon graduation, a large majority of NUS students will have received no training in mediation. These students are unlikely to receive instruction in properly understanding the mediation processes nor will they be familiar with its service providers unless they are exposed to them through internships or pro bono opportunities. The overall emphasis on litigation and its outcomes, coupled with the comparatively weaker emphasis on collaborative dispute resolution, implicitly conveys the message that collaborative forms of dispute resolution are less common and/or less important, and are merely *alternatives* to the default approach of conventional court-based dispute resolution.[44] This impression may be repeatedly reinforced over the many courses during a student's time in law school, resulting in a subliminal yet powerful bias in favour of the litigation paradigm that is difficult to detect and correct.[45]

III. What next?

In light of the foregoing discussion, it is submitted that if NUS is to remain relevant in developing the 21st century lawyer, the curriculum must be realigned with the reality of legal practice and the needs of the wider community. Calls have been made for Singaporean lawyers to undergo a mindset change to think "ADR" instead of "litigation or settlement",[46] and what better way is there to kick-start this change than for schools to inculcate this mindset in their students? As we prepare to ride the waves of mediation, it is vital that NUS, "which has already achieved so much, is ready to meet the future".[47] Conversely, it would be shortchanging students (and those students' future clients) if NUS does not improve its training to encompass the evolving role of lawyers by promoting and providing training in collaborative dispute resolution.[48]

Ideally, NUS' compulsory curriculum should include a course on mediation, which ensures that all students are trained in identifying interests instead of only identifying legal rights and positions. Incorporating mediation into the core curriculum will hopefully not only mitigate the extent to which students form a bias towards litigation in their foundational years, but also encourage them to pursue collaborative problem-solving methods wherever possible. The benefits of including mediation in the law school curriculum have been appreciated overseas as well. The National Alternative Dispute Resolution Advisory Council in Australia, the Law Council of Australia and Australian Council of Law Deans[49] have recommended that mediation be included as a mandatory part of the legal curriculum, and a survey of 27 Australian law schools revealed that 8 already had compulsory courses dedicated to other dispute resolution processes.[50] In a similar vein, the Legal Education and Training Review in the UK[51] has recommended that mediation should be a mandatory area of study for admission to practice.

That said, the workshop style in which mediation is taught places a premium on role-play exercises and constant bespoke feedback,[52] which makes an increase in the capacity of the mediation course impractical if the resources that NUS has to work with remain the same. Courses are capped to ensure quality learning and teaching outcomes, and to extend the offering to an entire cohort will require more financial support and manpower.[53]

However, even if NUS cannot train all its graduates in mediation, it can at least familiarise its students with the option of mediation in order to combat the instinct to think of litigation as the first port of call. This may be done by integrating avenues for mediation into other substantive law courses as part of how disputes in that area of law can be resolved amicably. For example, a tort case involving nuisance caused by one's neighbour might instead be resolved by mediation at the Community Mediation Centre, while contractual disputes may be resolved at the Singapore International Mediation Centre or the Singapore Mediation Centre. The hope is that by exposing students to the relevance of mediation across a wide range of courses, students will better appreciate its utility. This may also be incorporated into exams involving hypotheticals, where marks are awarded for identifying other appropriate forms of dispute resolution in the given scenario. Thus, even if students do not go in-depth into understanding the mediation process or the principles of mediation, they are at least aware of the process itself and its service providers. It would also be helpful if lecturers could provide insights into how disputes in that area of law have been mediated in the past, although this may be challenging if the lecturer has not spent time in practice.

IV. Conclusion

In conclusion, despite having achieved much over its history, now is not the time for NUS to rest on its laurels. Given how legal practice continues to change, it is important that NUS constantly reviews its curriculum in order to prepare its graduates for the future.[54] The point of this chapter is not to downplay the significance of traditional legal education that focuses on doctrine, deep analysis and advocacy, which remains important even with the increasing popularity of mediation. The perfect must not be the enemy of the good. Instead, this chapter must be seen against the backdrop of the larger conversation on what the role of a lawyer is, and how to prepare students for their vocation.

The move towards a holistic approach to dispute resolution,[55] both internationally and domestically, is best served by a holistic approach to legal education that trains lawyers to solve their clients' problems in a way that best meets the clients' interests. Improving NUS' curriculum is simply one approach towards effecting a legal cultural change that is conducive for this.

A Comparative Guide to Drafting Enforceable Mediation Clauses

Maryam Salehijam

I. Introduction

In our fast-paced world, commercial parties increasingly seek to prevent and resolve disputes in a cost and time effective manner. Their pursuit for a better way to resolve disputes led to re-emergence of non-binding (consensual) alternative dispute resolution (ADR) mechanisms in the 1990s.[1] Almost two decades later, the most prominent form of consensual ADR — mediation — enjoys global attention as dispute resolution providers,[2] policy makers and judges attempt to promote its use. Today, the promotion of mediation as the preferred alternative to litigation and arbitration has led dispute resolution providers and commercial parties to increasingly draft agreements containing multi-tiered dispute resolution (MDR) clauses[3] that call for mediation prior to other binding procedures.[4]

Although increasing resort to mediation as a result of these agreements is noteworthy, there is significant uncertainty regarding the binding nature thereof.[5] Such agreements have resulted in disputes about whether a party may ignore the agreement to mediate and proceed directly to binding mechanisms such as arbitration, the content of the parties' obligations (whether the parties must be physically present, attempt to settle, act in good faith, etc.), as well as the forum that may address the enforceability question.[6] Furthermore, the effect of mediation clauses on limitation periods, the validity of arbitral awards and subsequent proceedings is unclear.[7] The increasing litigation regarding mediation emphasises the need to clarify the enforceability of mediation clauses, as the current uncertainty compromises the benefits of this mechanism.[8] However, unlike in the case of commercial arbitration, the law on commercial mediation clauses is in its formative stages.[9] There is no uniform statute and rarely any legislative basis that addresses the consequence of the failure to comply with a mediation clause nor conditions for its binding nature.[10] Accordingly, national laws must be consulted in order to address the question of enforceability of such agreements.[11]

This chapter aims to give guidance to parties and dispute resolution providers interested in drafting enforceable agreements to mediate. It provides a new comparative perspective of the current approaches to the validity and enforceability of mediation clauses in selected states.[12] In the first section, a critical analysis of the current approaches to validity and enforceability is done. The second section, again using a comparative approach, assesses the manner in which such clauses are enforced trans-nationally by courts and arbitral tribunals. The final section provides concluding remarks.

II. Validity and enforceability

As is the case with arbitration clauses, mediation clauses should be viewed independently from the contract that contains them.[13] Therefore, the validity of mediation clauses is not affected by the invalidity of the main contract. Moreover, as mediation is a wholly different process than arbitration, the parties' agreement should not be assessed under the same conditions as the parties' agreement to arbitrate.[14] The doctrine of separability is supported on the basis of party autonomy, legal certainty, international comity and the policy to give effect to dispute resolution clauses.[15]

A. *Formal and substantive validity*

A valid mediation clause must be both formally and substantively valid. Formal validity relates to the external expression of the agreement.[16] Unlike arbitration clauses, to be formally valid, there are — with the exception of Singapore[17] — no special requirements outside of the applicable contract law requirements. Thus, mediation clauses do not have to be in writing or signed. Despite the lack of special form requirements, the parties should record their agreement to mediate in writing as proof of such an agreement.

The substantive validity of a mediation clause is a matter that can be affected by public policy and mandatory overriding rules, as the parties cannot escape these rules through contractual arrangements. The overriding mandatory rules and public policy of the place of mediation apply to the procedural, private and substantive law aspects of the mediation clause.[18] Hence, these mandatory rules apply regardless of a choice of law.[19] Public policy affects agreements that involve matters that cannot be subject to party autonomy, such as public administration and contracts involving third parties.[20] Of relevance here is the fact that the parties may not contract out of their inalienable right of access to justice. Nevertheless, in Germany, amongst many other civil law jurisdictions, the question of whether a mediation clause breaches the inalienable right (*unverzichtbares Recht*) "to a fair hearing with an impartial judge in accordance with the rules of natural justice" is answered negatively.[21] This answer comes in light of the view that such agreements are only a temporary waiver of the right to a fair hearing before a court or tribunal and not a permanent waiver of the right to access binding solutions.[22] This is in line with the ruling of the ECJ in the *Alassini*[23] case, where the Court acknowledged that the principle of a right to a fair trial may be subject to restrictions as long as these restrictions are proportionate and are part of a legislated public interest aim of improving access to justice.[24] Thus, the parties have the right to seek to resolve their dispute through an ADR mechanism.[25]

B. *The need for certainty and completeness/essentialia negotii*

For an agreement to be binding on the parties and thereby enforceable, it must in addition to being formally valid and without obvious errors, be sufficiently certain and complete (in civil law jurisdictions: *essentialia negotii*). The contract law requirement of certainty and completeness exists in many jurisdictions.[26] Certainty is essential to the enforcement of the clause, as the clause is not self-executing, and thus, courts need sufficiently objective criteria to assess parties' compliance with their agreement. Regarding certainty, it is of the essence to note that research on ICC tribunals indicates that they do not follow the judicial trend to assess the enforceability of mediation clauses. Instead, applying a two-pronged approach, the tribunals firstly tend to consider whether the parties had an obligation to attempt mediation prior to arbitration.[27] Parties must use mandatory wording to demonstrate the obligatory nature of their mediation clause.[28] If so, the tribunals, applying a factual analysis, check if this obligation was fulfilled.[29]

The following paragraphs provide an overview of the contrasting approaches to the enforceability of mediation clauses. In addressing the question of how courts apply the requirements of certainty and completeness, this chapter draws on a substantial body of case law from common law jurisdictions due to a lack thereof from civil law countries. The disparity in the number of cases between the common and civil law jurisdictions in focus is perhaps due to newness of commercial mediation in Germany and Austria.[30]

In addition, statutes in Austria and Germany do not regulate mediation clauses. Therefore, such agreements are regulated by general contract law requirements and the contents thereof are also left to party autonomy. For a mediation clause to fulfil the conditions for certainty, it must express the will of the parties to be bound by their obligation to mediate. In Germany, this can be demonstrated through *a pactum de non petendo*.[31] Alternatively, the parties can specify that the courts should dismiss claims brought in violation of their mediation clauses. In addition to expressing the will of the parties, an enforceable mediation clause must define the types of dispute the parties intend to submit to mediation.[32] However, it is not clear whether similar to common law jurisdictions, a specification of a procedure for the appointment of the neutral suffices in Germany or if the agreement must specify the mediator by name.[33] Nevertheless, it must be noted that in both jurisdictions the question of whether a mediation clause is enforceable has not yet been explicitly decided.[34]

Regarding the common and civil law divide to certainty, there is a philosophical difference to note. As evident, in the Germanic systems, the courts are attached to the notion that the will of the parties should be adhered to in order to ensure reliance and only the absence of will to enter into the contract should be a basis for avoidance.[35] The common law approach to protecting reliance, however, solely focusses on the binding nature of the contract. Moreover, amongst the common law jurisdictions in focus, there is a tendency to apply differing certainty thresholds. It appears that at this stage, the Australian and Singaporean courts take a more liberal approach than English courts.[36]

English courts have been criticised for their strict approach to sufficient certainty.[37] For instance, in 2012, in *Sulamerica*,[38] Moore-Bick LJ found the clause unenforceable while acknowledging that the parties clearly intended to be bound.[39] Likewise, Hildyard J in *Wah*,[40] found the clause unenforceable despite it establishing a detailed procedure, as the process was not clear regarding who was to be involved, whether the neutral was to reach a conclusion or take a particular step, and as the clause contained vague terms such as "attempt to resolve the dispute".[41]

The approach in *Sulamerica* and *Wah* seems to act against the 2002 celebrated judgement in *Cable & Wireless*[42] where Colman J of the Commercial Court found a clause enforceable despite the parties' failure to choose a particular method of dispute resolution.[43] This strict approach remains despite *Emirates*,[44] where a MDR clause requiring "friendly discussions" was found to be enforceable, as Teare J purposefully distinguished *Sulamerica* and *Wah* on the basis that these cases required mediation/conciliation while the clause in *Emirates* required the resolution of the dispute through friendly discussion in good faith. However, it is possible that the reasoning of Teare J will indirectly affect the courts' policy towards enforcing mediation clauses.[45] This is because English courts' main argument for their aversion to enforcement of these clauses has been their similarity to agreements to agree, which were prior to *Emirates* found to be unenforceable. Thus, it can be said that the position of English courts towards the enforceability of such agreements is evolving, while the approach to mediation clauses in Australia and Singapore can be summarised as enforcement friendly.

Although the approaches of Australian and Singapore are similar, with the passing of the 2017 Mediation Act (MA), Singapore appears to be a step ahead of Australia in its approach to mediation clauses. Article 8 of the MA grants Singaporean courts the statutory power to order a stay of proceedings pending a mediation as long as the parties have expressed their intention to be bound in writing. Accordingly, the MA does not appear to require the agreement to address further details about the procedure of mediation or the provider. The pro-enforcement policy of Singapore is also evident in case law. In *International Research Corp*,[46]

Sundaresh Menon CJ on appeal agreed with the High Court that the pre-condition to arbitration was enforceable although the title of the clause called for mediation, but described the process of negotiations.[47] Chan Seng Onn J of the High Court in relying on the mandatory character of the dispute resolution clause relied on the reasoning of Colman J in *Cable & Wireless* and did not make a reference to *Sulamerica* nor *Wah*.[48]

Likewise, the Australian courts' approach to dispute resolution clauses is to hold the parties to the terms of their agreement.[49] These courts interpret such clauses in a liberal way and thus in the same manner as other clauses in commercial contracts.[50] According to Vickery J in the Australian case of *WTE:*

"[A]s a minimum, what is necessary for a valid and enforceable dispute resolution clause, is to set out the process or model to be employed, and in a manner which does not leave this to further argument."[51]

Yet, the requirement of certainty does not imply that the dispute resolution clause must be overly structured.[52]

(1) *The good faith barrier*

In addition, the countries under analysis have differing approaches to whether a reference to a good faith obligation in the mediation clause warrants its unenforceability.[53] It seems that here the lack of consensus bypasses the common and civil law divide. English courts have been traditionally hostile to the doctrine of good faith.[54] The reluctance to recognise the duty of good faith follows a main principle of contract formation in the common law. Nevertheless, there appears to be a trend towards recognising the good faith obligation in dispute resolution clauses. Again, the English approach is worthy of criticism, as good faith is an accepted obligation in other common law jurisdictions.

C. *Ensuring sufficient certainty*

As evident from the earlier discussion, there is no uniform test to determine whether a mediation clause is binding on the parties. Courts approach enforceability in the majority of jurisdictions on a case-by-case basis. It seems that English courts are the most strict regarding contractual certainty principles, as a valid agreement almost has to refer to a dispute resolution centre to ensure certainty.[55]

Furthermore, there remains the reality that courts are likely to find an agreement to be unenforceable if it is missing minor details such as how the neutral is to be selected or remunerated. For instance, in the Australian case of *Aiton,* the mediation clause was found to be unenforceable as it failed to address the remuneration of the mediator.[56] Erlank argues that the court's refusal to order a stay on the basis of a missing mention of the mediator's fees "seems to be a bit hard and not conducive to a just result."[57] He rightly bases this argument on the fact that there are other ways in which the fees to be paid could be determined, such as those used in cases involving arbitration. Furthermore, there are court sponsored mediation programs that may guide the courts in assessing the remuneration of the mediator. In applying such a high threshold, the courts appear to act against the true intention of the parties in concluding agreements.

Today, in the absence of a uniform framework regulating the conditions for validity and enforceability of mediation clauses, it is important that the parties carefully draft their agreement in order to ensure its effectiveness. For a mediation clause to be binding regardless of the jurisdictions seized, it must indicate the parties' intention to be bound to the mediation by using mandatory language.[58] In common law jurisdictions, the parties must also clarify that the binding nature of the agreement is a condition precedent to other binding mechanisms.[59] Furthermore, it should address the following points:

   i. *How to initiate procedure*
  ii. *The scope of the agreement (disputes covered)*
 iii. *Applicable procedural and substantive law*
 iv. *Applicable institutional rules (attention must be drawn to the version agreed to)*
  v. *Description of the procedure*
 vi. *Procedure to select neutral(s)*
vii. *Parties' obligations*
     a. *Attendance obligations*
     b. *Behavioural obligations (cooperate, meaningful discussions, etc.)*

c. *Temporal obligations (minimum number of sessions or hours)*
   d. *Etc.*
viii. *How costs are to be divided/determined*
 ix. Consequence for failure to comply (stay, dismissal, damages, sanctions, etc.)
  x. *Place of mediation or method for selection thereof*
 xi. *Language of mediation or method for selection thereof*
xii. *Procedure to terminate mechanism*

ADR agreements that refer to the rules and procedures established by ADR institutions often meet the above underlined requirements. Nevertheless, parties should always make sure that the version of the mediation rules they are referring to are in fact covering aspects they have not included in their agreement.

III. Conclusion

Although commercial parties increasingly include mediation clauses in their commercial contracts with the aim of amicably and efficiently resolving their disputes, such agreements can have opposing effects. In reality, it runs contrary to practice to expect that dispute resolution clauses be extremely detailed. Practitioners and scholars frequently refer to dispute resolution clauses as "midnight clauses" since they are often concluded so late in the day. This is problematic, as it raises the chance of the agreement being poorly drafted. Therefore, there is a probability that a mediation clause concluded hastily might not fulfill the enforceability criteria. This is especially evident in cases where the party requesting the enforcement of a mediation clause is refused on the basis of an incomplete or uncertain clause. Unmistakably, there is a need for a new approach to these agreements that empowers the courts to fill the gaps in the parties' agreements in order to interpret in favour of enforcement. This suggestion is in line with the modern approach to interpreting commercial contracts, which is to give meaning to the terms in order to preserve validity, as long as the parties' agreement is formulated in mandatory terms. This is not to say the courts are to rewrite the contract for the parties.

Enforcing Mediation Settlement Agreements: An Examination of the Draft Convention on International Settlement Agreements Resulting from Mediation

Chia Chen Wei

> *"And noble offices thou mayst effect*
> *Of mediation, after I am dead,"*
>
> — King Henry IV, Part II
> (4.4.27-28)

I. Introduction

The history of mediation is long and distinguished — kings and leaders alike often depended on it as a tool to peacefully resolve conflicts.[1] Just as mediators in the past brokered alliances and coalitions between states, modern mediators repair relationships in the fields of commercial, family and labour law. It is thus unsurprising that international mediation surged in popularity ever since the dispute resolution revolution of the 1970s and 1980s.[2]

The UNCITRAL Working Group II's attempt to prepare a Draft Convention on International Settlement Agreements Resulting from Mediation ("**the Convention**"), while admirable, is not flawless. This chapter will examine the substantive provisions of the Convention in Section II, focusing first on the scope of the Convention's application, and secondly on the enumerated grounds for a refusal to grant relief. Recommendations for changes to the wording or substance of specific articles will be provided. Subsequently, Section III will evaluate the

34   *Contemporary Issues in Mediation Volume 4*

potential impact of the Convention on both international mediation practice worldwide as well as in Singapore.

II. Substantive provisions of the Convention

The Convention's purpose is to provide states with "consistent standards" to address the cross-border enforcement of international mediation settlement agreements ("**iMSAs**"),[3] thereby promoting greater use of international mediation as an effective tool for resolving cross-border disputes.

This section will focus on the Convention's substantive provisions, namely those that relate to the rights of parties in international mediation. It will examine Article 1, which relates to the scope of the Convention's application, and Article 4, which sets out the grounds for refusal to grant relief.

A. *The Scope of application — Caught between a rock and a hard place*

(1) *Explanation of Article 1*

Article 1 confines the Convention's scope to settlement agreements that resolve commercial disputes.[4] Article 1(3)(a) further excludes the Convention's application to settlement agreements that:

> (a) Have been approved by a court, or have been concluded before a court in the course of proceedings, either of which are enforceable [in the same manner] as a judgment [according to the law of the State of that court]

Under Article 1(3)(a), the competent authority of the state (State A) where enforcement was sought would determine whether a settlement agreement was enforceable in the same manner as a judgment in the State where court proceedings began (State B).[5] This determination was to be made in accordance with the law of State B, where the settlement agreement was approved or court proceedings took place. Further, a settlement agreement would be "approved by a court" or "concluded before a court" if it was reached with court assistance — for instance, settlement agreements reached during court proceedings but not recorded as judicial decisions would fall within the ambit of being "approved by a court" or "concluded before a court".[6]

The purpose of Article 1(3)(a) was to exclude from the scope of the Convention settlement agreements approved or concluded before a court in order to avoid possible overlaps with other existing or future international instruments;[7] the Working Group was particularly mindful of the Hague's upcoming Convention on judgements.[8]

(2) *Criticisms*

It is submitted that purposefully confining the scope of the Convention in the manner of Article 1(3) is flawed because: (a) it creates a significant gap in the law; and (b) it is doctrinally unsound to do so.

(a) Creation of a significant gap in the law

Article 1(3), in seeking to avoid overlaps with existing and future conventions, inadvertently creates a significant gap in the law. According to Article 1(3)(a), a settlement agreement that is enforceable as a judgement at the place of origin, but cannot be enforced as a judgement at the place of enforcement would be excluded from the scope of the instrument, thereby depriving parties of recourse for enforcement.[9]

This would be a minor problem if the vast majority of states ratified international conventions for cross-border recognition and enforcement of court judgements, such as the Convention on Choice of Court Agreement ("**CCCA**"); the latter allows for the court judgements of a member state to be enforced by another member state as if it were a judgement of the latter, subject only to narrow exceptions like fraud.[10] If so, the framework of the CCCA would suffice in allowing parties to enforce iMSAs.

However, to date, there are only 7 states parties to the CCCA — far from the widespread ratification of other international instruments such as the New York Convention ("**NYC**"), which has 157 states parties.[11] Thus, until a significant number of states ratify the CCCA, parties with iMSAs that are enforceable as court judgements would likely be unable

36   *Contemporary Issues in Mediation Volume 4*

to avail themselves of a multi-lateral enforcement instrument for ease of enforceability. Incidentally, this explains why Article 1(3)(b), which relates to the exclusion of iMSAs that are enforceable as arbitral awards, is less of a problem (due to the preponderance of states that have ratified the NYC).

(b) Doctrinal unsoundness

Moreover, it is doctrinally unsound to differentiate between settlement agreements on the basis of whether they are recorded by, or reached with the courts' assistance. iMSAs between the parties are, first and foremost, contracts. As was observed by the learned Judge Parke in *Wentworth v Bullen*, "The contract of the parties is not the less a contract...because there is superadded the command of the Judge."[12] Denying a party the right to utilise an international convention for mediation simply because the will of a judge is "superadded" is unintuitive and unjust.[13]

(3) *Recommendations*

The better approach would be to grant an innocent party autonomy in selecting between the use of the Convention, or other multi-lateral conventions such as the CCCA.

Nevertheless, one must recognise that the Working Group has evinced strong intentions to preserve this provision, even despite articulated concerns regarding the gap-creating effects of Article 3(1)(a).[14] Given this, it may be more appropriate to argue for the position in Article 1(3)(a) to be tempered, rather than wholly changed.

Thus, Article 3(a) should be modified such that where there are alternative avenues for the enforcement of an iMSA, it will be a strong factor that militates against the application of the Convention, but is not itself determinative of the Convention's exclusion.

Should the Working Group decide to address practical concerns specifically relating to the Convention's efficiency, a mechanism should be adopted for the state of origin to issue a certificate stating that the settlement agreement is enforceable in the same manner as a judgement in the state of origin;[15] this would avoid lengthy and complex inquiries into the enforceability status of settlement agreements in foreign states.[16]

B. *Grounds for refusing to grant relief — balancing flexibility and regulation*

(1) *Explanation of Article 4*

Article 4 of the Convention lays several grounds under which a state may refuse to enforce iMSAs. These include[17] (a) incapacity; (b) the non-binding or non-final nature of the settlement agreement; (c) the incapability of performing the settlement agreement under the law to which the parties have subjected it or under the law deemed applicable by the state; (d) a serious breach by the conciliator of standards applicable, without which breach that party would not have entered into the settlement agreement; and (e) a failure by the conciliator to disclose circumstances to the parties that raise justifiable doubts as to the conciliator's impartiality or independence that had a material impact or undue influence on a party, without which failure that party would not have entered into the settlement agreement.

Key problems lie within Articles 4(1)(c), 4(1)(d) and 4(1)(e).

(2) *Criticism of Article 4(1)(c)*

Under Article 4(1)(c), a state may refuse to grant relief if the settlement agreement is deemed incapable of being performed under the law to which the parties have subjected it. The ambiguity in the wording of "incapable of being performed" means that this provision could potentially extend to situations where the law is silent on whether a particular act or measure may be performed or enforced. If so, then the convention would end up "stifling, instead of accommodating, the creativity that is inherent in the mediation process".[18]

In mediation, the terms of settlement agreements need not focus solely on a restricted range of legal remedies.[19] Given the inherent flexibility of mediation processes in accommodating a wide range of stakeholders in ways that more formal processes such as arbitration and litigation do not normally allow,[20] it is likely that the unique solutions found in iMSAs may not be expressly provided for under national legislation. For instance, the terms of an iMSA may include a public apology by a party (akin to the concept of accord and satisfaction),[21] or a change in certain company policies to appease one's employees.[22] Such terms are likely to satisfy parties to a mediation, as such parties are often individuals who have their particular internal issues superimposed on the corporate point of view,[23] but will rarely be contained in written law.

The lack of express provision in national legislations for novel solutions in dispute resolution is more likely to be a problem in common law jurisdictions, because the enforcement of such solutions is likely to be seen as something akin to specific performance.[24] Common law jurisdictions typically discourage, or refuse to recognise specific performance as an enforced measure or remedy, instead preferring to award monetary compensation.[25] Conversely, civil law jurisdictions like Germany and France more readily accept specific performance as a method that satisfactorily fulfils the agreement of parties, as may be seen from Section 611 of the German Bürgerliches Gesetzbuch,[26] and Article 1184(2) of the French Civil Code.[27]

Thus, Article 4(1)(c) may compromise the efficacy of the Convention if states refuse to enforce iMSAs simply because certain terms or measures are not recognised or provided for under their national legislation. This would in turn negatively impact party autonomy and flexibility by constraining the range of solutions reached in a settlement agreement.

(3) *Recommendations for Article 4(1)(c)*

It is important to emphasise that the above criticism only applies if the following two conditions prevail: (1) the wording of "may refuse to grant relief" under Article 4(1) is read as a mandatory exhortation for the relevant authorities of states parties to automatically deny relief once the settlement agreement is "incapable of being performed under the law"; and (2) where the law is silent on a particular measure, that measure may fall within the scope of being "incapable of being performed under the law".

While the plain wording of "may refuse" appears to unequivocally indicate that states parties possess the discretionary power to enforce iMSAs even when they fall within the scope of one of the enumerated grounds, this is not so. The phrase "may refuse" is borrowed from Article V of the NYC; this phrase has generated considerable debate over whether the courts of states parties are obligated to automatically refuse the enforcement of arbitral awards once one of the enumerated grounds are satisfied.[28]

Thus, the Working Group should make explicit in their wording of Convention Article 4(1)(c), whether states parties preserve a discretionary power to enforce iMSAs. Additionally, clarificatory notes on the ambit of the phrase "incapable of being performed under the law" would also alleviate any uncertainty surrounding this provision.

(4) *Criticism of Articles 4(1)(d) and (e)*

Articles 4(1)(d) and (e) suffer from the same problem — the party making an application for the denial of relief has to furnish proof that "without which" breach or failure of the conciliator to maintain certain standards or disclose circumstances, that party would not have entered into the settlement agreement.

There is thus a requirement of causation to be proved, apart from showing a manifest failure by a mediator to observe certain standards of conduct, which would already be difficult to establish given the confidential nature of mediation, a party has to further show that "but for" the mediator's breach, he or she would not have entered into the settlement agreement. While the grounds for refusing to grant relief should be narrow so as to preserve the validity of iMSAs in the vast majority of circumstances, this ground places too onerous an obligation on the party making an application.

(5) *Recommendations for Articles 4(1)(d) and (e)*

It is submitted that it would be sufficient for the party to show that it was materially prejudiced by the mediator's breach of his or her duties, rather than demonstrating the causative link between the mediator's breach and the party's entry into the iMSA. This is so especially considering that the failure of a mediator to remain impartial, or to disclose any potential conflicts of interest is a grievous one; where he or she has breached this duty of impartiality, there is a violation of natural justice.[29] Further, the sufficiency of showing material prejudice as a ground for invalidity has been recognised in both international commercial arbitration and investor-state arbitration.[30]

III. The potential impact of the Convention — boon or bane?

Having discussed several of the Convention's provisions, this chapter will now analyse the potential impact of the Convention in terms of the risks and opportunities that it offers for international mediation practice worldwide, as well as in Singapore.

A. *Risks*

The Convention presents two general risks: (1) the erosion of mediation confidentiality; and (2) the over-regulation of mediation practice. Additionally, specific to Singapore's Mediation Act, it discourages parties from recording their mediated settlement agreements as an order of court.

(1) *Erosion of mediation confidentiality*

The first risk posed by the Convention is the potential erosion of mediation confidentiality. The determination of whether an iMSA should be enforced will likely entail the disclosure of mediation communications and information related to the mediation proceedings,[31] especially in circumstances where a party argues that the mediation was tainted with mediator bias or partiality under Article 4(1)(d) or (e).

The premium that parties place on mediation confidentiality was acknowledged by UNCITRAL in its guide to the 2002 Model Law on International Commercial Conciliation, where it stated that "the single most important concern of parties in conciliation is to ensure that certain statements or admissions made by a party in conciliation proceedings will not be used as evidence against that party in other proceedings".[32] This potential erosion of mediation confidentiality may dissuade parties from engaging in international mediation.

(2) *Discouraging the recording of settlement agreements*

The presence of Article 1(3)(a) of the Convention, which excludes from the scope of the Convention settlement agreements that are enforceable as a judgement, discourages the use of Section 12 of the Singapore Mediation Act, which allows parties to record their settlement agreement as an order of court.

Section 12 was intended as an "additional, expedited way" for parties to ensure the enforcement of their iMSA through the recording of their agreement as a Singapore court order;[33] however, doing so would exclude this very agreement from the scope of the Convention. The parties would thus be faced with a dilemma over whether to use the machinery of the Mediation Act, or the Convention; this would naturally discourage the use of Section 12.

B. *Opportunities*

(1) *Encouraging international mediation*

On the other hand, it can be argued that the Convention encourages the use of international mediation through its presentation of an international, harmonised framework for enforcement of iMSAs. As shown in an International Mediation Institute survey from 2014, approximately 93% of respondents would be more likely to mediate a dispute with a party from a country that ratified a UN Convention on the enforcement of iMSAs.[34] The presence of such an international enforcement mechanism thus motivates parties to engage in international mediation in the first place. This is especially significant, given the lack of enforcement options specific to cross-border mediation. The rise of international mediation would likely benefit Singapore, given its continual efforts to position itself as a dispute resolution hub through processes such as Arb-Med-Arb.[35]

Moreover, while current trends demonstrate the widespread practice of parties voluntarily abiding by their iMSAs, it would be erroneous to assume that this pattern of conduct will remain. Prevention is better than cure — the Convention would guard against any future trends of reneging parties.

(2) *The erosion of mediation confidentiality — merely a myth?*

While not technically an advantage, the aforementioned erosion of mediation confidentiality may not actually occur.

It must first be acknowledged that in jurisdictions such as Singapore, legislation mandating the disclosure of mediation communications in select circumstances is already in force; Singapore's Mediation Act provides a multifactorial test with factors such as public interest and the administration of justice for deciding whether mediation communications should be disclosed.[36]

Additionally, disclosure is likely to be the exception rather than the norm. Courts are unlikely to order disclosure merely because a party alleges bias or partiality on the part of the mediator as the strength of the party's case will first be examined. International commercial arbitration, which similarly places a premium on party confidentiality, proves instructive in this regard. Despite the NYC being in force for more than 50 years, arbitration's reputation as a bedrock of privacy and confidentiality remains.

C. *Evaluation — returning to the Wild West?*

As shown earlier, the Convention is likely to bring both risks and opportunities to the sphere of international mediation. It must be emphasised that the question before the international community is not whether mediation should be regulated, but rather, how to appropriately regulate it.[37]

Mediation is a wholly different beast from arbitration. While reference and inspiration may be taken from the NYC, the regulation of mediation must be done in a manner that respects its flexible and unique nature.

Author's Note: While the information relating to the provisions of the Draft Convention was accurate at the time the chapter was submitted for publication (5th April 2018), the draft Convention has since been published as the "United Nations Convention on International Settlement Agreements Resulting from Mediation", and will, when the signing ceremony for the Convention is held in Singapore on 7 August 2019, be known as the "Singapore Convention on Mediation".

Mediation Obligations and Ethics

Mediator Neutrality in Singapore: The Siren Call for a Paradigm Shift

Kuek Kai Liang

I. Introduction

It is undisputed that the current ethical paradigm in mediation is based around the notion of mediator neutrality. Definitions of mediation often refer to mediators as neutral interveners with accompanying codes of conduct making frequent references to mediator neutrality.[1] At the outset, it is acknowledged that while various models of mediation are practiced,[2] the focus of this chapter is the facilitative model of mediation.

Disturbingly, the achievement of neutrality has been described as "impossible", with empirical studies showing the absence of mediator neutrality in any absolute sense.[3] Consequently, mediator neutrality has been argued to be an aspirational concept. The problematic notion of mediator neutrality is compounded when one realises how inept this fabled notion is at dealing with power disparities present in mediation.[4] Hamstrung by neutrality, mediators compromise a party's capacity for self-determination — the core value of mediation.

The aforementioned problems have resulted in calls for an ethical paradigm shift away from mediator neutrality towards a more nuanced and contextual approach to mediation ethics.[5] This chapter is a humble attempt at providing an answer to the problems that plague the current ethical paradigm. It argues that the answer lies in a paradigm shift towards contextual ethics — the heart of which is the core value of relational party self-determination. The adoption of contextual ethics will be explored in the Singapore context, with a discussion of possible alterations to the Singapore International Mediation Institute Code of Professional Conduct ("SIMI Code") to reflect thereof.

II. Neutrality and its attendant problems

The problems plaguing neutrality are two-fold. First, neutrality is theoretically attractive but practically impossible and therefore purely aspirational. Second, where power disparities arise, the mediator is faced with the unenviable dilemma of either adhering to neutrality at the expense of self-determination or vice versa.

A. *The notion of neutrality*

While mediator neutrality is not unequivocally defined, there are two generally accepted meanings of neutrality. First, the neutral mediator is *disinterested* in the content or outcome of the dispute.[6] Second, the neutral mediator is *impartial* in that he is even-handed in his equal treatment of the disputing parties.[7]

These meanings of neutrality comport with the "outsider-impartial" role the facilitative mediator is supposed to play.[8] He merely facilitates the mediation process without influencing the dispute's content or outcome which are self-determined by the parties. Additionally, he practices impartiality by giving equal attention to each party without displays of favouritism.

It is apt to emphasise that facilitative mediation was, in part, developed as an alternative to the adversarial system where parties surrendered control of their dispute by having a decision imposed on them.[9] In light of this, the ethical paradigm is based on the neutral mediator allowing parties to reach a self-determined, uncoerced outcome.

B. *Neutrality is practically impossible and purely aspirational*

Neutrality may be affected by both the mediator's conscious and unconscious processes.[10] Neutrality is possible where the mediator has no prior relationship with either party nor a vested interest in the outcome of their dispute. In these situations, the mediator is consciously aware that he merely facilitates the process without any incentive to influence content or outcome.

However, it is the mediator's unconscious process that has insidious effects rendering neutrality practically difficult, if not impossible.

Mediators, like all persons, are inevitably affected by individual values, beliefs, cognitive and motivational bias. Whilst facilitating the process, the mediator may unconsciously act on these biases, influencing the content or outcome of the dispute.

The preceding discussion has led to a recognition that the distinction between process and content or outcome is practically unrealistic.[11] In facilitating the process, the mediator frames the discussion and distributes the parties' opportunities to speak. The influence on content or outcome via the mediator's process interventions manifest in subtle ways. One such example is selective facilitation. This occurs when the mediator frames the discussion in a manner which advances a "preferred" outcome and induces compliance thereof.[12]

The current ethical paradigm views neutrality through a binary prism: mediators are either absolutely neutral or not.[13] Consequently, *absolute* neutrality in the sense of disinterestedness in the content or outcome is practically impossible for they are inevitably influenced by process interventions. Since no mediator can ever be *truly* neutral, neutrality is alas, purely aspirational.

C. *The mediator's dilemma in power disparities: Neutrality or self-determination*

(1) *Power disparities in mediation*

It is useful to start with a discursion into the concept of power in mediation. Mediation requires the parties to negotiate effectively to attain a consensual outcome. Their ability to negotiate effectively is affected by the power relationship between them. First, this relationship is rarely symmetrical — some power disparity inevitably exists.[14] Second, the interactional nature of mediation means that power often shifts during negotiations and is a dynamic rather than static concept.[15]

(2) *Self-determination and mediation*

In the context of mediation, self-determination is understood in a relational sense. Relational party self-determination is achieved where the mediator facilitates *both* parties in reaching an outcome that addresses the needs and interests of not just one, but *both* parties.[16] It bears emphasis that relational party self-determination is *the* quality that makes mediation different from other dispute resolution processes and is consequently *the* core value of mediation.[17]

(3) *The mediator's dilemma*

The current ethical paradigm prescribes neutrality as a means to an end — upholding the parties' self-determination.[18] Theoretically, the means achieve the end when the parties' consensual and uncoerced agreement is made possible via the mediator's impartial and equal treatment.

Theory assumes that there is little or no power disparity between the parties.[19] Following the discursion earlier, theory, unfortunately, does not accord with practice. Mediation often involves strategically superior parties refusing to budge from positional-based tactics or parties with the propensity to threaten or intimidate, pitted against relatively inferior or meeker disputants. Even when the parties are relatively equal in terms of strategic or personal power, one party may attain disproportionate power over the other as the power shifts during negotiations.

The mediator's dilemma inevitably arises where power disparities exist. If the mediator acts in a completely impartial manner, he perpetuates the existing power dynamics resulting in an outcome that reflects the needs of the relatively more powerful party. Thus, only one party achieves self-determination and the outcome is hardly consensual. Yet, the mediator is no longer neutral if he behaves partially towards the weaker party in addressing the power disparity. Ultimately, power disparities force the mediator to choose either upholding relational party self-determination *or* adhering to neutrality.[20]

Empirical studies provide an insight into how mediators deal with this dilemma. Mediators often address power disparities via process interventions — for example, distributing more opportunities to speak to the less articulate or weaker party.[21] At times, they intrude upon the content or outcome during caucuses and reality testing.[22] Ultimately, they either assert neutrality but intervene regardless, or refrain from intervention whilst expressing discomfort with a rigid adherence to neutrality.[23]

D. *The need for an ethical paradigm shift away from neutrality*

The legitimacy of the mediation process is founded on the notion of neutrality.[24] Legitimacy is questioned when mediators effectively misrepresent themselves as "neutral facilitators" whilst practicing partiality, consciously or otherwise. Furthermore, despite neutrality being the supposed means to the core value of party self-determination, instances of power disparities demonstrated its ineptitude at offering ethical guidance for achieving the end.[25] If anything, neutrality is a means that has gotten in the way of achieving the very end it had promised. This calls for a new ethical paradigm.

III. The case for an ethical paradigm shift towards contextual ethics

Contextual ethics essentially require the decision-maker's assessment of the context of the situation in which decisions are made.[26] Ethical decisions are made based on whether they are contextually *appropriate* rather than right or wrong as dictated by rigid rules.

A. *Contextual ethics in mediation*

Since relational party self-determination is *the* core value of mediation, contextual ethics require the mediator to consider all relevant circumstances of the particular mediation in deciding how to best uphold party self-determination.[27] The relevant circumstances will necessarily include power disparities and shifts in power, and consequently whether mediator intervention is appropriate.

Intervention is appropriate where power disparities become disproportionate such that one party's self-determination is under threat. The context of such situations entitles the mediator's partial treatment of the weaker party in furtherance of obtaining an outcome that reflects relational party self-determination.

Contextual ethics requires the mediator to be "omnipartial" in that he is on both parties' sides as opposed to impartial where he is on no party's side.[28] The mediator's focus is not on his impartiality, but on the attainment of a self-determined "win-win" outcome. This entails the possibility of partial treatment in favour of *either* party at different points of the mediation, if the circumstances so require. Partial treatment is paradoxically fair and thus, even where the mediator is not completely even-handed, he *does not* unfairly advantage one party at the other's expense.

B. *Contextual ethics offers a better way to support parties in mediation*

The ethical paradigm of neutrality represents a rule-based approach to mediation ethics.[29] Its rule-based nature is glaringly deficient in offering guidance in the support of parties attaining self-determination.[30] Rule-based neutrality requires a strict adherence to neutrality or impartiality for that is the "right" ethical decision. Regardless of circumstance, a deviation from the rule is "wrong".

This binary categorisation of ethical decision-making leaves little or no room for actual decision-making on the mediator's part.[31] The default "right" decision of remaining impartial renders rule-based neutrality impotent in dealing with the ever-changing context that follows the relational and interactive nature of mediation. The mediator is effectively put in a straightjacket because he would be "wrong" to address power disparities and shifts in the power dynamics as it requires a deviation from the rule. To "rightly" remain impartial at the expense of upholding parties' self-determination, despite the former being the means to the latter, explains the mediator's dilemma. The existence of the dilemma is testament to the failure of neutrality as an ethical guide in supporting parties in mediation.

Contextual ethics dispenses with the binary categorisation of the rule-based approach, representing a nuanced approach that offers guidance where neutrality has failed. Without the default "right" decision, mediators are free to make actual decisions in response to power disparities and shifts in power dynamics. The responsiveness to the realities of mediation practice is guided by the mediator's imperative to uphold the core value of mediation — relational party self-determination.[32] This guided responsiveness is practical, not aspirational, consequently offering a better way than neutrality in supporting parties in mediation.

IV. Addressing the primary concern regarding contextual ethics in mediation

Interestingly, the non-rule-based quality of contextual ethics that allows its responsiveness to reality is the very same quality that has engendered concerns. The primary concern is that, without a rule-based compass, contextual ethics amount to no more than unprincipled, "anything goes" ethics.[33] It is imperative to address this concern to make a truly persuasive case for an ethical paradigm shift towards contextual ethics.

A. *Relational party self-determination — the lodestar*

If it follows the lodestar of relational party self-determination, contextual ethics in mediation can hardly be described as "anything goes". Therefore, contextual ethics does not grant the mediator a license to intervene in *any* way he sees fit, especially if parties appear to reach an outcome he does not prefer. As relational party self-determination is directly related to the attainment of consensual and collaborative outcomes,[34] mediator intervention is ethically inappropriate if it intrudes upon such outcomes.

It is imperative that mediators recognise that the responsibility for the dispute's outcome lies with the parties. Thus, a mediator should not make substantive decisions on behalf of a party, even when said party is negotiating at a clear disadvantage. Even in the face of power disparities, *overt* outcome interventions like pressuring a party to reach an agreement are contrary to relational party self-determination and are ethically inappropriate.[35]

B. *Informed consent — the imperative*

Instead, contextual ethics will require power disparities to be addressed via process interventions within a framework supporting informed consent. It is imperative that an outcome is not merely the product of consent, but of *informed* consent, for *genuine* relational party self-determination to be achieved.[36]

There are many process interventions suited for the different contexts from which power disparities arise. Mediators may use reality testing to

52 *Contemporary Issues in Mediation Volume 4*

determine if a more emotionally engaged and therefore vulnerable party is making an informed decision.[37] Should there be information asymmetry, informed consent may require non-prescriptive advice or adjourning the mediation pending legal advice. If the power disparity is unacceptably disproportionate, for example where the weaker party is intimidated and lacks capacity for informed consent, the mediation may be appropriately terminated.[38] A focus on process interventions with a concurrent recognition of informed consent prevents contextual ethics from becoming "anything goes" ethics.

C. *The community model of ethics*

The community model is one where the professional community, rather than its regulatory bodies, bears primary responsibility for mediation ethics.[39] This model requires mediators to reflect on their responses to ethical situations and discuss these experiences with others in the community. Over time, a collection of responses in varied situations shape the ethical discourse and may even be codified. Such collegial accountability is not as utopian as it seems, as is evident by both American and Australian model standards mirroring the community model.[40]

The community model complements existing regulatory codes and is well-placed to guard against the slide of contextual ethics into "anything goes" ethics. Fears stemming from a lack of rule-based guides are allayed as ethical judgements under the community model are, instead, guided by values that evolved organically and internally within the profession.[41]

V. Embracing contextual ethics in Singapore

A. *How would contextual ethics differ from Singapore's current ethical paradigm?*

The current ethical paradigm in Singapore's mediation landscape is reflected in the SIMI Code, the Singapore Mediation Centre Code of Conduct ("SMC Code") and the State Courts of Singapore: Code of Ethics and Basic Principles on Court Mediation ("State Courts Code"). In accordance with the codes, the current ethical paradigm in Singapore's mediation landscape reflects an almost single-minded commitment to mediator neutrality.

Pertinently, explicit references to neutrality are found in all three codes. For instance, the SIMI mediator is referred to as a third-party neutral. It is apt to observe that the SMC Code has no reference whatsoever to the core value of relational party self-determination while the SIMI Code contains only implicit references thereto.[42] The State Courts Code, however, does explicitly mention a similar concept of "empowerment" as a core principle.[43]

With reference to the codes, contextual ethics differs from the current ethical paradigm in that the codes do not adequately emphasise relational party self-determination nor address features like informed consent, power disparities and the community model.

B. *Possible alterations to the SIMI Code*

Embracing contextual ethics in Singapore would entail significant changes to the codes. It is thus apt to discuss possible alterations to the SIMI Code, with inspiration drawn from the National Mediator Accreditation Systems Practice Standards ("NMAS Practice Standards") and the US Model Standards of Conduct for Mediators ("US Model Standards").

First, the SIMI Code should include an explicit endorsement of relational party self-determination. The definition of mediation in the code should reflect that "mediation is a process that promotes the participants' self-determination."[44] Alternatively, an explicit codification of party self-determination as an ethical principle may be included.[45]

Second, Clause 5 of the SIMI Code, titled "Mediation Process", should include a sub-clause requiring the mediator to remain cognisant of power disparities and to manage shifts in power dynamics accordingly.[46]

Third, Clause 5.8 of the SIMI Code — requiring the mediator to ensure that in the outcome of an agreement, said agreement is done voluntarily and with the consent of all parties — should be altered to include "informed consent" instead of mere consent.[47] Additionally, a sub-clause requiring mediators to, where appropriate, refer participants to sources of information or advice should be included under Clause 5.[48]

Fourth, Clause 2 of the SIMI Code, titled "Promotion of Mediation Practice" should include a sub-clause encouraging mediators to engage with the mediation community in terms of peer consultation and learning.[49] This recognition of the community model should include the explicit goal of improving the profession to better serve its clients.[50]

Lastly, Clause 4 of the SIMI Code, the explicit neutrality clause, should be amended to ensure neutrality is not a strict rule-based requirement. Mediator neutrality should be explicitly subject to "variable circumstances of the particular mediation" such as power disparities mentioned in the amended Clause 5.

VI. Conclusion

It bears emphasis that the ethical paradigm of neutrality is merely a means to the end that is relational party self-determination. Yet the problems that plague neutrality render the means unable to serve the end it promised. Since neutrality is fast losing relevance as a legitimising function of mediation, the need for an ethical paradigm shift is a pressing one.[51] The practice of contextual ethics, keeping the lodestar, the imperative and the community model in mind, is principled and far from "anything goes" ethics. Consequently, if relational party self-determination is the prince that was promised, contextual ethics is the horse on which he rides.

The Case for Confidentiality: Singapore's Mediation Act

Nadene Law Qin Ning

I. Introduction

At first glance, confidentiality conferred on mediation communications seems absolute. Besides the fact that it is often touted as a key tenet of mediation,[1] mediators frequently give parties unqualified assurances of the confidentiality of the proceedings.[2] Yet, a careful look into the law reveals lapses in the protection offered by mediation confidentiality.

This essay seeks to evaluate the importance of confidentiality in mediation and the degree to which it should be protected. To that end, the scheme regulating mediation confidentiality in Singapore will be assessed. Special attention will be paid to the newly enacted Mediation Act (MA),[3] insofar as its enactment offers an opportunity to re-evaluate Singapore's framework for protecting mediation confidentiality. It will be shown that, while the MA is a step in the right direction, the current state of law in Singapore vis-à-vis mediation confidentiality is unsatisfactory and should be strengthened through the adoption of "almost absolute confidentiality".

Part II evaluates the importance of mediation confidentiality and analyses competing considerations in determining the scope of protection that should be afforded. Part III then examines the regime in Singapore governing mediation confidentiality and shows how the current state of law leaves much to be desired, even with the advent of the MA. Part IV explores the viability of enacting a general mediation privilege in Singapore as a solution. It is suggested that the legislature should take guidance from the United States' Uniform Mediation Act by entrenching a mediation privilege in Singapore's MA.

II. Importance of mediation confidentiality

Confidentiality is generally thought to be critical to a successful mediation process.[4] This is likely rooted in the nature of mediation, which envisions parties having an honest discussion about the issue at hand, and aims to preserve ongoing relationships or make the termination of the relationship less acrimonious even if parties fail to arrive at an agreement.[5] Thus, the more candid parties are about their needs and interests underlying their positions, the higher the likelihood of finding a satisfactory resolution.[6] In this manner, the cloak of confidentiality facilitates free and honest disclosure.

A. *To what extent should mediation communications be protected?*

Yet, the extent to which mediation confidentiality should be protected has been open to considerable debate.[7] This section will show that mediation communications are key to mediation proceedings, such that they should be afforded absolute protection, save in cases where justice necessitates a compromise.

(1) *Arguments for the absolute protection of mediation communications*

(a) Confidentiality is required to facilitate full and frank discussions

The most common argument for absolute mediation confidentiality is that it is required to create an environment that facilitates full and frank discussions between the mediator and the parties respectively, as well as between the parties.[8]

Two key factors play a role in facilitating full and frank discussions: the creation of an atmosphere of trust and the protection of the mediator's status as a neutral, both of which are fostered by confidentiality.[9]

Without trust and the assurance that communications would be kept confidential, parties are less likely to disclose private information to the mediator. This is especially since parties might perceive a risk that the mediator would reveal this information to the other party and place them in a disadvantageous position.[10]

The same rationale applies to the parties *inter se*. Parties are encouraged to speak freely among each other with the assurance of confidentiality since this promotes an atmosphere free of "restraint and intimidation".[11] Conversely, the lack of the protection of confidentiality may inhibit negotiation.[12] Parties might be reluctant to disclose information that is potentially useful for settlement discussions because of the perceived risk that such information may be used against them in later proceedings.[13] This attitude of wariness is fuelled by the litigation mindset, which is observed when parties have resorted to mediation in an attempt to settle pending or threatened litigation.[14]

Further, mediation confidentiality protects the mediator's status as a neutral third-party through the recognition of a mediator's privilege not to testify in court.[15] If a mediator testifies in court against the interests of a mediating party, he will likely no longer be perceived as impartial, regardless of how objective his testimony is.[16] Accordingly, a mediator's privilege promotes a mediator's neutrality since there would be no risk of him being a potential adversary in later litigation.[17]

Thus, the promise of confidentiality ensures that parties trust the mediator and are willing to speak freely amongst each other. Without such assurances of confidentiality, the potential effectiveness of mediation would quickly diminish.[18]

(b) Confidentiality protects party autonomy

Mediation confidentiality also protects party autonomy and the freedom of independent decision-making,[19] which is especially pertinent where a settlement does not eventuate and parties decide to litigate instead. Without confidentiality, parties may be able to adduce evidence of statements made within the mediation context. It is unfair to hold parties to statements made in a non-adversarial context, since the preservation of the relationship and common interests of both parties which are central to mediation are no longer prioritised. Confidentiality is thus important so that parties can "adopt any position they wish in mediation and subsequently change their position without detriment should the matter proceed to arbitration or litigation".[20]

(2) *Arguments against the absolute protection of mediation confidentiality*

Nonetheless, it is acknowledged that there are several counter-arguments militating against the absolute protection of mediation communications through confidentiality.

(a) Courts should have access to the best possible evidence

The most common counter-argument is that absolute confidentiality would hinder future litigation in the event the mediation process does not yield a settlement. Mediation confidentiality at its broadest sacrifices potentially important evidence for subsequent legal proceedings and restricts public access to information that may be necessary to a democratic society.[21] Thus, courts have primarily justified the breach of mediation confidentiality by reasoning that it would ensure the availability of the best possible evidence in court proceedings, and in turn increase the likelihood of attaining a fair, just and legal outcome.[22]

(b) Parties may abuse absolute mediation confidentiality

An attendant concern of not having the best possible evidence available is the fear that parties will abuse absolute mediation confidentiality. Parties should not be allowed to take advantage of confidentiality by being able to sterilise potentially damaging evidence through deliberately introducing that evidence in mediation with the sole purpose of preventing it being introduced as evidence in a subsequent hearing, even if the subject is irrelevant to the mediation.[23]

Further, parties may use the cloak of confidentiality to evade responsibility of being held to a settlement. It is submitted that allowing an advantage of mediation to be manipulated as a tool to evade lawful consequences would be antithetical to the spirit of mediation and justice as a whole.

The pressing risk of abuse is also seen with regard to the actual or threat of the commission of offences and crimes. It seems absurd that a legal process can be used to harm, rather than to protect. Allowing such abuse to occur would not foster confidence in the mediation process given that confidentiality would be seen as a potential cloak for mediator misconduct.[24]

(c) Lack of empirical evidence supporting necessity of confidentiality in mediation

The last point seeks to rebut the argument that confidentiality is necessary for an effective mediation. Many academics have argued that this may not be so, in light of the lack of empirical evidence indicating that confidentiality is necessary for the success of the mediation process.[25] In fact, an empirical study showed that clients do not necessarily confide all relevant information to their lawyers despite the existence of lawyer-client privilege.[26] While the study is not directly relevant to the effectiveness of mediation privilege, one may analogise the two privileges and conclude that similar difficulties may plague a mediation privilege and defeat the purpose of protecting confidentiality in the first place. Further, there are limitations to the scope of confidentiality, as well as risks associated with mediator assurances that everything said by parties in mediation will remain confidential — mediation cannot be used to hide information that would otherwise be legally discoverable.[27]

(3) *A compromise — almost absolute confidentiality*

Having canvassed both sides of the debate, it appears that there is a tension between the administration of justice[28] and the preservation of the integrity of the mediation process.[29] It is submitted that a compromise can and should be reached for the sake of conceptual and practical coherence in mediation.

In determining the optimal approach to finding a compromise, one should consider three main categories of protection for mediation communications:

(a) Absolute confidentiality, whereby no disclosure of any mediation communications may be made;

(b) Almost absolute confidentiality, which prioritises confidentiality except in cases of enumerated exceptions; or

(c) Qualified confidentiality, which recognises the importance of mediation confidentiality but provides judicial discretion to order disclosure in individual cases where needed to prevent a manifest injustice or to enforce court orders.[30]

It is submitted that an optimal balance is struck through recognising almost absolute confidentiality with its clearly identified exceptions. The alternatives are unpalatable: absolute confidentiality leaves no room for flexibility even where injustice occurs, whereas qualified confidentiality poses a risk that judicial discretion will be exercised arbitrarily, and thus unjustifiably encroach on the protection of sensitive information. Almost absolute confidentiality, on the other hand, provides a more just solution by identifying discrete instances where the rigid adherence to absolute confidentiality would result in manifest injustice, while ensuring that the mediation process is not unduly impinged upon by infelicitously-worded provisions giving judicial discretion.

Further, the arguments against mediation confidentiality are not substantiated. First, while there is admittedly no empirical support for the proposition that confidentiality is absolutely essential to facilitate an effective mediation, it cannot be gainsaid that generally, people are less willing to share information with people they do not trust. Second, while confidentiality potentially prevents access to the best evidence available, the need to preserve relationships within the mediation context is sufficiently important to justify relative inaccessibility to such evidence although they may be required for the unwavering pursuit of truth-finding.[31] This is especially in light of processes provided by litigation, such as discovery.

Therefore, if one accepts that there is still a need for mediation confidentiality, it is submitted that mediation confidentially should be protected in an "almost absolute" manner. Protection of confidential information should be given as a starting point and should only be attenuated in discretely identified situations where considerations of justice militate in favour of disclosing the information.

III. Mediation confidentiality under the Mediation Act

Bearing in mind the desirability of almost absolute confidentiality, this chapter turns to examine the extent to which the MA gives effect to the tenet of confidentiality. It is imperative to briefly outline the regime that governed mediation confidentiality before the enactment of the MA and the problems faced.

A. *Before the Mediation Act*

Before the MA was enacted, mediation confidentiality was governed by a combination of common law rules and specific statutes.

(1) *Mediation confidentiality in the common law*

The common law recognises three types of confidentiality: (a) legal professional privilege; (b) contractual confidentiality and (c) Without Prejudice privilege.[32]

(a) Legal professional privilege attaches to confidential communications brought into existence for the primary purpose of existing or contemplated legal proceedings, and aims to protect the client's rights should litigation ensue.
(b) Contractual confidentiality arises when parties to a mediation sign express agreements to protect communications arising from that mediation.
(c) Without Prejudice privilege applies to protect communications that seek to settle an existing or contemplated dispute between parties to the mediation.

Thus, it appears that there exists a comprehensive and sound web of mechanisms that work alongside each other to protect mediation confidentiality. However, all three forms of privilege have either been eroded by the development of common law exceptions, are arguably inapplicable to the mediation context or can be easily defeated:

(a) As regards to legal professional privilege, it is questionable whether Ramsey J's proposition in *Farm Assist (In Liquidation) v Secretary of State for the Environment, Food and Rural Affairs* that legal professional privilege should extend to mediators is good law in Singapore.[33] In any event, it is arguably incongruous to ascribe a characteristic of the lawyer-client relationship to the mediator-party relationship, given that the lawyer is seen as an advocate for his client, while a mediator is supposed to be a neutral third party to the dispute.

(b) Contractual confidentiality can be easily lost insofar as contracts restricting use of evidence in judicial proceedings are liable to be found "void as against public policy".[34]

(c) The law on Without Prejudice privilege recognises a plethora of exceptions.[35] This reneges on the promise of absolute protection seemingly afforded to mediation communications.

(2) *Mediation confidentiality in specific statutes*

In contrast, it is submitted that the protection given to mediation confidentiality in specific statutes is relatively high. For example, Section 19 of the Community Mediation Centres Act evinces commitment to confidentiality in community mediations, by rendering "evidence of anything said or of any admission made" non-admissible "in any proceedings before any court, tribunal or body".[36]

The common law types of confidentiality also feature in certain statutes. For example, Section 23(1)(a) of the Evidence Act (EA) gives effect to contractual confidentiality by excluding admissions if they were made "upon an express condition" that evidence of it would not be given.[37] The Without Prejudice rule appears to be represented under Section 23(1)(b) of the EA, insofar as its wording allows parties to argue that communications during mediation were made with the intent of resolving the dispute amicably without any recourse to litigation, such that these communications were never intended to constitute evidence.[38]

Legal professional privilege is also provided for under Section 128 of the EA.[39] However, unlike the other provisions, there are express exceptions where legal professional privilege does not apply, mainly where communications have been made in furtherance of an illegal purpose, or where statements relate to facts that show that any crime or fraud has been committed. As outlined earlier, it is unclear whether legal professional privilege does or should extend to mediators.

B. *After the Mediation Act*

In comparison to the regime laid out earlier, it is submitted that the MA improves the protection of mediation confidentiality in three aspects:

(a) The MA affords mediation proceedings a high level of protection, as evidenced by the wide definition of "mediation communications".[40]
(b) The MA gives effect to party autonomy by permitting disclosure with the consent of the parties, and rightly excludes the mediator in attaining consent for disclosure unless the statement sought to be disclosed was made by that mediator.[41] This difference in treatment is justified, given that the mediator has no personal interest in a statement that is made by one of the parties.[42]
(c) The MA promotes mediation confidentiality as a rule rather than exception, as seen from how it declares all communications confidential, subject to the listed exceptions.[43] This optimal approach is reinforced by the existence of only ten exceptions that expressly give persons the right to disclose mediation communication to a third party to the mediation.

Yet, there are multiple problems inherent in the approach adopted by Singapore. The most glaring issue is the fragmented nature of Singapore's regulation of mediation confidentiality. The application of the MA is limited to private mediations that are connected to Singapore.[44] This results in three separate regimes governing mediation confidentiality, which is unfair to parties since the amount of protection given to their communications is determined by something as arbitrary as the regime under which their mediation proceedings falls. There is no reasonable justification for the different treatment of disputes that may result in equally severe consequences.

An additional problem stems from the existence of additional exceptions to mediation confidentiality under Section 9(3) and Section 10 of the MA. Disclosure to third parties is permitted with the leave of a court or tribunal in four situations,[45] while mediation communication can be admitted as evidence in court with leave of a court or tribunal if the court is satisfied that it is necessary.[46] This discretion is guided by factors which inform the court of matters that must be taken into account in deciding whether to allow disclosure.[47] Although it can be argued that the requirement for leave guarantees an additional layer of protection, the court's wide discretion is troubling. The language is vague and does not offer any actual guidance as to what the limits of disclosure should be.[48] Overly broad and simply worded confidentiality provisions may do unintended harm notwithstanding the salutary purposes for which they were enacted.[49] This poses a severe threat to mediation confidentiality in Singapore.

Still, all is not lost. The fragmented regulation of mediation confidentiality can be easily remedied through Section 6(3) of the MA, which allows the Minister to make future orders to extend the application of the MA to mediations conducted by the courts. However, the threat posed to mediation confidentiality by the court's unnecessarily wide discretion as provided for in Section 11 of the MA requires a more drastic solution: the adoption of an almost absolute mediation privilege in Singapore.

IV. Designing a mediation privilege for Singapore: Suggestions for increased protection of mediation confidentiality

Almost absolute privilege is a moderate form of protection for mediation communications — it is subject to enumerated exceptions, which significantly limits the scope of the court's discretion to allow a breach of confidentiality.[50] The United States' Uniform Mediation Act (UMA) provides a good example of this.[51] It is submitted that the confidentiality and privilege provisions in the UMA should be adapted into the MA.

Section 4 of the UMA provides differentiated privileges for mediation participants and affords the broadest privilege and ability to prevent disclosures to the parties.[52] Exceptions to the mediation privilege are seen in Section 6 of the UMA which provides detailed and express requirements for disclosure. The confidentiality and privilege provisions of the UMA affirms principles important to mediation such as party autonomy, while simultaneously striking a desirable balance between promoting mediation itself while ensuring considerations of justice are not ignored. For example, the UMA recognises instances where disclosure is required where there are pressing considerations of justice, or where there is danger posed to an individual.[53]

It is acknowledged that the UMA appears to give the court a similar type of discretion afforded to Singapore courts in the MA.[54] However, it can easily be distinguished from the discretion conferred on the courts in the MA in that the UMA limits the discretion by discrete requirements.[55] The UMA discretion is also subject to an extra layer of protection, by only permitting "the portion of the communication necessary" to be admitted if it falls under the exception.[56] This serves as a reminder to the court and the public of the importance of confidentiality in mediation proceedings.

V. Conclusion

The enactment of the MA reflects Singapore's commitment to becoming a dispute resolution hub.[57] In view of this, it is critical that no stone be left unturned to ensure that mediation is regarded as a dispute resolution mechanism on the same plane as litigation and arbitration. The best way to do this is to protect the integrity of the mediation process by prioritising confidentiality, a key pillar of mediation. The MA represents a good starting point, given that it significantly protects mediation communications. However, given the potential danger engendered by the wide discretion given to the courts in Section 11 of the MA, amendments should be made to expressly identify those situations where information will not be protected as being confidential. Until then, the MA is a welcome — albeit imperfect — development that provides added assurance to mediators and participants alike vis-à-vis mediation confidentiality in Singapore.

A Review of Mediator Neutrality

Ivan Ng Yi Fan

I. Introduction

Neutrality is widely considered to be one of the sacred pillars of a practice in mediation.[1] Yet, this supposedly indisputable requirement is not without controversy. In fact, mediator neutrality as a concept has been lambasted by critics since the inception of mediation[2] and the debate is still raging on today. In view of the confusion surrounding mediator neutrality, it is imperative that mediators and mediation organisations understand what it actually requires of them practically. This chapter will first consider some understandings of neutrality and its associated problems. The chapter then explores how neutrality interacts with some other values in mediation before wrapping up with some suggestions of how neutrality as a concept (and its interaction with other values) in mediation practice can be clarified.

Firstly, this chapter does not argue for the removal of neutrality in mediation. Neutrality as a general concept on the part of a third party arbiter is crucial to the success of any conflict resolution; simply imagine a scenario where a mediator favours one party/child over another in the event of a dispute. At best, the party discriminated against may not trust the mediator and refuse to be forthcoming or cooperative during the dispute resolution process. At worse, gross injustice will be carried out. Therefore, some measure of neutrality is desirable and should be expected on the part of mediators. At the same time, neutrality as an absolutist concept is an impossible goal.[3] Humans naturally hold biased tendencies and views depending on their experiences or held values and it is impossible to expect mediators to be completely objective and impartial. While efforts should certainly be undertaken to help mediators rid themselves of some of this internal bias,[4] requiring mediators to be completely neutral is simply unrealistic.

II. Unpacking the meaning of neutrality

If it is impossible for one to be "completely neutral", it begs the question: "what aspect of neutrality should we then hold mediators to?" Part of the reason why there is such controversy over mediator neutrality is because there is little consensus on what the word "neutrality" means and mediators or mediation codes of conduct are unclear on its definition. This chapter will introduce four possible ideas of what "neutrality" in mediation may mean, as surfaced by Susan Douglas in a study on mediator perceptions of neutrality.[5]

Firstly, there is neutrality as *impartiality*; the mediator must have no vested interest or a conflict of interest in the mediation and must guard against the potential intrusion of their personal reactions or preferences.[6] The benefit of mediator impartiality is relatively straightforward. No husband in an estranged marriage would want to participate in a mediation where the mediator is the wife's friend and whom does not like him, or whom is a judge known to favour wives over husbands in family proceedings, or whom is the wife's employee and receives their payroll from the wife. In each of these scenarios, the mediator is in a position of conflict of interest or whom has much vested interest in an outcome that favours the wife. On the other hand, an impartial mediator encourages the parties to negotiate as well as share information with the mediator with the trust that the mediator will not take sides between the parties.[7] However, as mentioned earlier[8] people naturally have subjective tendencies and while it is ideal for a mediator's personal reactions or preferences to be reined back, this is not always possible. Nevertheless, obvious situations of conflicts of interest or vested interests should be avoided as far as possible for neutrality as impartiality to be attained.

Secondly, there is neutrality as *even-handedness* means that the mediator seeks to create an even playing field procedure-wise during the mediation.[9] He ensures that the process does not unduly favour one party over the other and gives both parties as equal attention as possible.

This is related to neutrality in terms of a *distinction between process and content*. As the mediator in the scenario attempts to equalise the mediation process, he controls the procedure but remains neutral or disinterested in the substantive outcome.[10] This is also known as the distinction between procedural justice (or the process of the mediation) as opposed to substantive justice (or the result of the mediation). While mediators are called to ensure the former, they are generally restrained from interfering in the latter to prevent their own subjective preferences from influencing the parties' autonomy and choices.[11]

Neutrality as even-handedness and the distinction between process and content is largely concerned with procedural fairness during the mediation. For example, this can be in the form of giving the parties equal time to air their concerns against the other party, equal opportunities for private meetings or simply giving an even amount of attention to both parties. Whether parties choose to use the equal opportunities that have been granted to them is their prerogative; the main point is that the mediator has treated the parties equally procedure-wise. This also ties in neatly with neutrality as impartiality because an impartial mediator who does not hold a preference for one side over the other should strive to treat both sides equally during the mediation process. Unfortunately, it has been observed that mediator intervention in the process of mediation does "influence both the content and outcome of the parties' dispute",[12] especially during reality testing. This means that the process-outcome distinction cannot be cleanly cut and even mediators who strive to be even-handed sometimes end up influencing the substantive outcome of the mediation, or at the very least struggle with uncertainty and dissatisfaction with the need to remain neutral.[13]

III. Neutrality as self-determination

The final concept of mediator neutrality as enabling party *self-determination* deserves a section on its own due to its complexity. Under this concept, the mediator refuses to be the one designing the solution; he instead encourages the parties to take the lead to come up with their own agreement. In this way, the mediator wants the parties to have ownership of the agreement,[14] literally "making it theirs" by putting them in control of the decision-making process.[15] The mediator acts simply as a facilitator and cheer-leader, not a lawyer or judge, and this neutrality allows the parties to autonomously come to a settlement on their own thereby legitimising the entire mediation process (as the mediator has no authority to decide for the parties). Therefore, self-determination through informed decision-making can be considered the lynchpin that holds mediation together[16] and in an ideal situation, the various forms of mediator neutrality allow parties' self-determination to freely and fairly come to a negotiated agreement. Naturally, parties are also more likely to comply with a settlement that they have willingly constructed on their own and in which they hence have a personal stake in. However, this necessitates that parties *actually* have the autonomy, necessary information and an environment where they can exercise that self-determination effectively. Unfortunately, that is not always the case in practice.

In a mediation, parties are rarely, if ever, equal. This inequality between parties can occur in a variety of non-exhaustive ways; power imbalances in terms of negotiating power, one party having more information or withholding it from the other party, representation by legal counsel (or the lack thereof) or aggressive/intimidation negotiation tactics. Of course, most mediators are already aware of such issues and resort to methods such as reality testing or even termination of the mediation session if they see the need to deal with a particular problem that is affecting the parties' autonomy.[17] However, the problem with this is that in doing so, the mediator has already failed to remain neutral and is effectively using strategies to influence the outcome.[18] For example, a mediator might decide to ask an abused party in a family mediation to seek a counsellor to assist her in the mediation as the abusive party would otherwise continue to take advantage of her emotionally-abused state. Or a mediator may privately request for one party's lawyers to reassess the party's legal options because the mediator has expertise in that area and has noticed that the lawyer has not adequately prepared for the mediation session, thereby providing their client with lacklustre legal advice. A mediator may also check privately with a party whether she really wants the offered settlement and if she is aware of alternative options, if the settlement amount is drastically below what she would have attained otherwise. While the methods in these examples arguably further party self-determination by ensuring that they are making considered and informed decisions, they clearly favour one party over another (probably the party with less power/information/representation/aggression) and thus contravene various concepts of mediator neutrality. Therefore, neutrality has to take a backseat on some occasions if self-determination is to be achieved, especially if it is considered that self-determination is the lynchpin that legitimises mediation in the first place. Even commentators who argue for neutrality to be retained recognise that neutrality in process must sometimes be compromised[19] for procedure to be fair and just in order for parties to make effective decisions.[20]

IV. Neutrality and (in)justice

The conflict between party self-determination and neutrality reveals an important fact that neutrality does not exist in a vacuum but interacts with other objectives and goals in mediation. Codes of conduct for mediators also reflect these other values.[21] In fact, it is arguable that the debate over mediator neutrality is not so much about how neutrality is defined as much as how it interacts with these other objectives such as fairness, justice or self-determination.[22]

It should be fairly clear that neutrality, if taken literally and in an uncompromising way, can become a vehicle for injustice (consider the same examples of inequality in the section on neutrality as self-determination earlier). Therefore, there is a possible case for justice being a more important goal that takes precedence over neutrality when these values conflict in some cases. Yet, justice is also an amorphous and problematic term. Does justice refer to substantive or procedural justice? Who decides what is justice?

Some commentators have taken the stance that as long as mediators remain neutral to the substantive outcome of the mediation but apply procedural rules so that the parties' deliberations are given effect to (thereby fulfilling party self-determination) the "resulting outcome will be just".[23] This is essentially an expansion of the concept of neutrality as a distinction between process and outcome and the mediator's own perceptions of substantive justice are taken out of the picture. In its place, the parties' view becomes the yardstick by which justice or fairness is measured and "public legal norms" become merely relevant rather than definitive.[24]

That said, apart from the practical difficulty of distinguishing between the process and outcome of the mediation, it is also arguable if mediators should really just ignore the outcome irrespective of how substantively unjust it may be. There are already situations beyond which some form of substantive justice is considered. For example, mediators are required to terminate the mediation if parties are "attempting to obtain an unfair advantage" or "pursuing an illegal or improper purpose".[25] The paramount interest of the child is also a substantive consideration that mediators must give precedence to during family mediation sessions.[26] It is particularly interesting that the court has powers to refuse a mediated settlement agreement on substantive grounds.[27] While some of the reasons under which a court may do so are similar to issues that go to a parties' self-determination in making decisions, such as fraud or duress, others lie at the substance of the mediation agreement itself, for example under the Mediation Act (MA), Section 12(4)(b), (c) and (d) determines if the subject of the agreement is capable of settlement, enforcement by order of court or against the best interests of a child. Even more broadly, under Section 12(4)(e) of the MA, the court can refuse to record a mediation settlement if it is contrary to public policy. Considering that the court itself looks to the substance of the agreement to determine if it should be enforced, crafting an agreement that is unenforceable in court is contradictory to the stance that mediation settlement agreements are binding on the parties involved, with repercussions if they choose not to adhere to the agreed terms.

Further, this chapter argues that some basic level of substantive fairness should be sought in a mediation settlement apart from merely ensuring that settlement agreements do not fall foul of applicable law. In a scenario where one party is at a disadvantage (or even when parties are on a level playing field), it is likely that they would prefer a mediation process where some minimal level of substantive fairness is guaranteed to grant them some assurance and protection.[28] Also, even if a mediator tries to make the procedure as fair as possible and pushes for party self-determination, much still turns on the parties' own psyche and negotiation or even emotional capacity. This appeal to basic/minimal substantive fairness thus acts as a *safety net* for parties who are simply unable to consider the substantive criteria for themselves, allowing mediators to discuss substantive issues with parties in a candid manner or even call an end to the mediation to protect the parties. It is imperative that even while considering the terms of the agreement substantively, mediators are not to take on the mantle of judges and force parties towards terms that the mediator thinks is optimal. On the other hand, rubber-stamping unconscionable agreements simply because one's client says so enacts a far greater price by eroding justice itself. A possible compromise might be for the standard for mediator intervention to be extremely high and triggered only when substantive justice is so absent that it shocks the conscience. This is in contrast to the Australian National Mediation Accreditation System (NMAS) Standards which arguably endangers neutrality too much by allowing mediators to terminate a mediation as long as they view that the mediation is no longer "suitable or productive"[29] or if the agreement is merely "unconscionable".[30] Such a standard would encroach too much into the parties' self-determination and does not consider that there may be considerable latitude in the views between parties and the mediator within which the parties' wishes should take precedence, rendering the mediator someone akin to that of an absolute arbiter.

V. A way forward for neutrality

This chapter has briefly canvassed some forms of neutrality as well as how they interact or conflict with other values in mediation such as self-determination or justice. It is argued that a review of local mediation standards should be conducted to clarify what "neutrality" actually means as well as how it should interact with these other values, especially as other codes of conduct differ on these points.[31] Some key clarifications and changes are proposed:

1. *Self-determination* is the key concept undergirding mediation. Mediator neutrality (or any derogation from neutrality) should hence seek to advance party self-determination.
2. Mediators should be as *impartial* as possible and avoid situations of conflict of interest or vested interests. Mediators should also strive to rein in their subjective bias during a mediation and should undergo specialised training to do so.[32]
3. Mediators should be as *even-handed* as possible and ensure procedural fairness during the mediation process. However, this will be overridden by the need to ensure party self-determination.

4. Mediators must be neutral as to the substantive *outcome* unless said outcome is unconscionable to the point where it shocks the conscience or falls foul of the provisions under Section 12(4) of the MA, as the court may refuse to record the settlement as an order of court anyway.

Even while considering these clarifications, it must be reiterated that mediator neutrality is an essential component of mediation and must never be removed entirely. However, an insistence on neutrality while ignoring its definitional problems or the ways it interacts with other values is detrimental to mediation as a dispute resolution process. It may result in mediation settlements that are unenforceable in court and also confuses mediators who end up relying on "societal norms and personal values" instead of varying results to similar fact patterns.[33] Most importantly, it has the potential to take away the autonomy of parties, the lynchpin of mediation, or cause substantive injustice to the parties involved. Naturally, the changes proposed here are not meant to be exhaustive or final and further discussion is called for to determine the mediation standards we want to see locally. Nonetheless, it is hoped that a process where mediators can think about neutrality in a more structured and practical manner can be started, rather than have an amorphous cloud of "neutrality" hang over mediator's heads in their course of work. Eventually, clarifications should be made to the local mediation standards and guidelines as well as taught to current and upcoming mediators. Let us solve this long-debated quagmire once and for all so that mediators can more effectively help their clients with a proper framework of neutrality in mind.

The Ethical Boundaries of Honesty in Mediation

Lew Zi Qi

Suppose you are a mediation advocate representing a divorcee in a mediation. At stake are the division of matrimonial assets, and care and control of the child. Your client does not want care and control, but he has advised you that the counterparty desperately wants it. He encourages you to lie (to the mediator and the counterparty) that he wants care and control so that you may use the issue as leverage for the division of matrimonial assets. To assuage your conscience, you tell yourself that this is merely the initial position to play "hardball". You are sincere in wanting to reach an agreement and will concede care and control after you have made the most of the leverage. Is the lie ethically acceptable?[1]

From the perspective of a mediation advocate, I will argue that the answer to the above question is "no",[2] but that lying in some circumstances in a mediation is ethically acceptable to advance the client's interest.[3] Ethics aside, the decision whether to lie or not will also depend on one's approach to mediation and negotiation. For example, a mediation advocate trained in the integrative school of negotiation or the facilitative school of mediation will probably emphasise the interest-based bargaining and non-adversarial nature of mediation,[4] and regard lying as distasteful. On the other hand, some lies *within ethical boundaries* may (but not necessarily) find a more receptive audience with proponents of a distributive bargaining approach to negotiation.[5] Even a mediation advocate who may normally shy away from lying may be tempted to lie if by that lie his client stands to gain a large advantage during mediation, particularly if the client is cognisant of this fact and encourages it, as in the earlier divorce example. After all, a lawyer's instinct to get the best outcome for his client does not magically cease at mediation. Regardless of one's approach to mediation, the purpose of this chapter is to provide an ethical, rules-based framework for the mediation advocate to navigate the grey area between getting the best deal for his client and his duty of honesty during mediation. Specifically, this chapter examines whether it is ethically permissible for the mediation advocate to lie in some contexts to get the best deal for his client.

Although lying often carries a negative connotation, in this chapter it simply means creating an untruth, whether by a positive act or omission. At heart is a tension between the mediation advocate's duty to advance his client's interests (which may involve lying), and his duty to the mediator and counterparty to act in good faith. I will first examine the duty of good faith and its contents as defined by case law and argue that good faith does not preclude certain types of lying.

Finally, I will explore the different types of lies that a mediation advocate may be tempted to make and examine their ethical permissibility in the context of the mediation advocate's duty of good faith.

I. The Yardstick

When we say that an action is "ethically acceptable", we base our judgement on a pre-existing normative theory of morality. People disagree on the bases of their ethical judgements, and much more the judgements themselves. It is beyond the scope of this chapter to venture into the epistemology of morality. It suffices to say for the purposes of this chapter that I will be using a deontological approach,[6] that is, an approach that considers the various ethical *duties* (a concept which, in its legal form, should be familiar to lawyers) that the mediation advocate owes to his client, the mediator and the counterparties. Ethical duties may clash, in this case the mediation advocate's duty to protect the interests of his client and his duty to act in good faith.

It is trite law that mediation advocates have a legal duty to act in good faith during mediation,[7] although the exact contents of that duty are less clear. A legal duty is not the same as an ethical duty, but the two frequently go together. In agreeing to mediation, the mediation advocate takes on a concurrent ethical duty to act in good faith as well. To put it the other way, the legal duty is the law's way of compelling the mediation advocate to discharge his ethical duty. It is what the mediator and counterparty expect of him, and it is what he has knowingly and voluntarily undertaken in convincing his client to go for mediation. I will be using the ethical and legal duties of good faith interchangeably.

A. *The contents of good faith*

There has been no local judgement on the contents of good faith in the context of a mediation. In *HSBC Institutional Trust Services (Singapore) Ltd (trustee of Starhill Global Real Estate Investment Trust) v Toshin Development Singapore Pte Ltd*,[8] the Singapore Court of Appeal ("SGCA") held that an express contractual clause directing contracting parties to "in good faith endeavour to agree on the prevailing market value" of certain premises was sufficiently certain to be valid and enforceable in law.

Although the case concerned a commercial contract, the SGCA also attempted at para [45] to consider the content of good faith "shorn of context" and cited an English judgment[9] that "the words 'in good faith' have a core meaning of honesty …". Later at [47], the SGCA further noted that "(t)he common threads connecting most attempts to define 'good faith' are fairness and honest dealing."

In summary, the SGCA seemed to think that the crux of the duty of good faith is to act honestly. Unfortunately, it did not elaborate on what it meant by "honesty", which can have a range of meanings in a mediation.

One meaning is that the mediation advocate must be genuinely committed to reaching an agreement with the counterparty, and not use the mediation process as a way to drag out proceedings. This form of honesty is synonymous with sincerity in committing to the mediation process itself (as opposed to honesty *during* mediation). In *United Group Rail Services Ltd v Rail Corporation NSW*[10] ("*United Group Rail Services*"), the New South Wales Supreme Court held at [15] that good faith requires parties to "endeavour genuinely to resolve a dispute". A lawyer that uses mediation to drag out proceedings rightly incurs the moral disapproval of the court. In practical terms, such behaviour will fall within a court's discretion as to costs under Order 59, rule 5 of the Rules of Court which permits the court to consider "the parties' conduct in relation to any attempt at resolving the cause or matter by mediation…". Therefore, the first ethical duty of good faith requires the mediation advocate to be honestly committed to mediation.

Another interpretation of honesty is that the mediation advocate must tell the truth during mediation. For example, suppose the mediation advocate is representing a client who is trying to get paid for services provided. He says, "$7,500 is the absolute lowest amount I can accept" when $7,000 is the lowest figure the client has given. Going by a strict literal interpretation of "honesty", his lie would put him in breach of his ethical duty to act in good faith. This would go against commonly (albeit not universally) accepted notions that some form of posturing or keeping one's cards close may be condoned in a mediation. On the other hand, a more egregious lie about a client's (fake) interest to get leverage (as in the case of the above divorce example) would be harder to justify. The point here is that there are different types of lies (which will be considered later) with different degrees of ethical controversy that may require a nuanced view of the requirement of honesty *during* mediation. Therefore, the second ethical duty of good faith requires the mediation advocate to be honest during mediation, but the exact boundaries of this duty is best considered with the different types of lies a mediation advocate may tell during mediation, which will be considered later.

B. *The duty to advance the client's interests*

A mediation advocate also has an ethical duty to advance his client's interest. There are two ways this duty may interact with the duty of good faith. The first is to say that the duty of good faith takes into account and accommodates the mediation advocate's duty to his client so that there is no conflict between the duties at all. This may be seen in the New South Wales Supreme Court's holding in *United Group Rail Services* that although the duty of good faith does impose "some fetter on the complete freedom" of the parties to the mediation, it does not require either party to "abandon" their own interests (at [15]). While conceptually neat, when taken as an ethical rule it seems to assume that the mediation advocate's duty to his client and duty of good faith will not be at odds, or if it does, that the duty of good faith should automatically take precedence.[11]

The more realistic position was stated in the Australian case of *Hooper Bailie Associated Ltd v Natcon Group Pty Ltd*,[12] where the court observed (at page [21]) that "there is a necessary tension between negotiation, in which a party is free to, and may be expected to, have regard to self-interest rather than the interests of the other party, and the maintenance of good faith". The difficulty is that where two ethical duties conflict, we need an adjudicating criterion to decide which duty should take precedence.

C. Types of lies

We are now ready to consider the various types of lies that a mediation advocate may be tempted to tell to protect his client's interests, bearing in mind the two meanings of honesty that form the content of the duty of good faith, namely (1) that the mediation advocate genuinely endeavours to resolve the dispute at mediation and (2) that the mediation advocate tells the truth during mediation.

(1) *Lies about a client's commitment to mediation*

In this scenario, the mediation advocate is lying about the client's sincerity in seeking a resolution to mediation. This may be because it is in the client's interests to drag out proceedings, especially where the client has deeper pockets to pay legal fees than the counterparty. (The perceived benefit of this strategy must be considered in light of the above-mentioned Order 59, rule 5 of the Rules of Court, which allows the court to consider the parties' conduct in relation to any attempt to resolve the dispute by mediation.) In practical terms, this may involve the "mediation advocate" deliberately advancing unreasonable proposals, constantly altering demands and shifting positions or even failing to attend a mediation session. This type of lie directly contradicts the first meaning of honesty in the duty of good faith.

Lawyers are often reminded that they are officers of the court first, and representatives of their clients second. The idea is that a lawyer's foremost duty is to serve the interests of justice. This duty does not lapse

80   *Contemporary Issues in Mediation Volume 4*

in the context of mediation, especially if the mediation is court-ordered or a preliminary effort to resolve the dispute before litigation.

The lawyer's duty to advance his client's interests does not override his duty to serve the interests of justice, or of intuitive notions of fair play, both "higher" ethical obligations which the duty of good faith protects. We must say that the first meaning of honesty in the duty of good faith is stronger than the duty the lawyer owes to his client's interests. It would be ethically wrong for a mediation advocate to lie about his client's commitment to mediation.

(2) *Distributive lies to gain an advantage during mediation*

The second category of lies consists of distributive lies which are intended to give the liar an advantage.[13] I will divide this category into lies about positions and interests. Briefly, "An interest is a motivation behind a position adopted by a party. It represents the needs, desires and concerns of the party. A position is merely one way to satisfy a perceived interest or set of interests."[14] Distributive lies clash with the second meaning of honesty in the duty of good faith, namely, that the mediation advocate should be honest during mediation.

A mediation advocate makes a positional lie when he states a more demanding position in anticipation that the counter party will attempt to bargain it down. To use the above example, a mediation advocate may say, "$7,500 is the lowest amount I can accept" when $7,000 is the lowest figure the client has given. Although the mediation advocate has a duty to be honest during negotiation, the extent to which he violates this duty has to be measured against the egregiousness of the lie he tells. To that end, padding one's position is a common negotiation tactic. To use a poker analogy, bluffing is an accepted part of the game. After all, parties often expect to have to make concessions from their initial position, especially if they subscribe to the distributive school of negotiating. Given that a positional lie is commonly expected by the other party in a mediation, the mediation advocate would be safe ethically speaking in following his duty to his client even at the expense of a technical breach in his duty of good faith.

Alternatively, it may even be suggested that this is a case where the two duties are not in conflict at all. To quote the court in *United Group Rail Services*, although the duty of good faith does impose "some fetter on the complete freedom" of the parties to the mediation, it does not require either party to "abandon" their own interests (at [15]). Seen in this way, the duty of good faith would accommodate positional lies.

Lies about interests are intuitively more egregious than positional lies. An example is the earlier divorce mediation example, where the mediation advocate lies that his client wants care and control over the child as leverage over the division of matrimonial assets. The question is whether this is subject to the same mitigating factor as a positional lie — that is, whether parties in a mediation generally anticipate the other party lying about his interests. Strictly speaking, this is an empirical question best answered by an anonymous survey of mediation parties which is an endeavour beyond the scope of this paper. I am content to leave it to the individual reader to decide his answer.

Should the mediation advocate choose to lie about his client's interests, he should take care not to violate the first meaning of honesty in the duty of good faith by advancing unreasonable proposals or constantly altering demands and shifting positions such that he is effectively undermining his client's sincerity in resolving the dispute. The mediation advocate should be ready to concede the (fake) interest before the mediation fails, and in perceiving when to concede the interest, he should err on the side of caution.

(3) *Lies about material facts*

While distributive lies deal with the client's positions and interests, lies about material facts cover all other lies about facts that the parties may consider in reaching an agreement. Such lies include lies about opinions and intentions,[15] all of which may amount to a misrepresentation under contract law. Furthermore, there is ethically speaking no difference between a positive act of lying and lying by omission, if the effect is to create an inaccurate picture in the counterparty's mind to induce him to enter into an agreement which he would otherwise not have.[16] Such a lie could potentially render any agreement reached void or voidable. It would

82   *Contemporary Issues in Mediation Volume 4*

in fact be a subset of a lie about the client's commitment to mediation itself (the first meaning of good faith), since such a lie would undermine the outcome of the entire mediation.

It would also violate the second meaning of good faith, i.e. honesty during mediation, except that unlike a lie about the client's position (which I have argued is ethically permissible), the counterparty will not generally expect lies about material facts. Unlike the litigation process, there is no procedure for fact-finding in a mediation and parties will expect their counterparties to come to mediation prepared to tell the truth about material facts. In this case, the duty of good faith should take precedence over the mediation advocate's duty to his client (it may not even be in the client's interest for the mediation advocate to lie about material facts. If the lie voids the agreement, the client is worse off than before the mediation, unless of course his interest is advanced by dragging out proceedings).

(4) *Lies with ethical implications outside mediation*

When a mediation advocate makes a lie affecting a third party outside of the mediation, the added ethical cost may cause the scale to tilt in favour of his duty of good faith. For example, the mediation advocate who lies about his client's interest in having care and control is using the child (and the other parent's love) as a bargaining chip in the mediation, an action that most people would find ethically odious. In Kantian terms, it would be using the child as a means to an end. In such circumstances, there is a compelling ethical duty (besides the duty of good faith) which trumps the mediation advocate's duty to advance his client's interests.

II. Conclusion

I have focussed on the two ethical duties that a mediation advocate will shoulder in his capacity as a mediation advocate, namely, his duty to advance his client's interests and his duty to act honestly in good faith. As the earlier discussion shows, it is usually in the client's interest for the mediation advocate to be honest. Furthermore, the only ethically permissible lies are lies about the client's position and (perhaps) interests, where such lies will give the client an advantage in mediation. Even then, the mediation advocate may choose to advance his client's interest in an honest, if less advantageous, way. However, for those lawyers who find themselves torn in the grey area between getting the best deal for their clients and honesty, it is hoped that this chapter provides a familiar rules-based framework to weigh the various ethical duties.

Mediation Skills

Negotiating with Children and How that Teaches Us to Be Better Mediators

Ho Ting En

I. Introduction

We often seek to improve our ability as mediators by learning from other adults, such as lecturers and authors. However, we may have failed to notice that one of the best learning opportunities come from interacting with children. While parenting articles and books increasingly advocate negotiation with children as a tool to teach them how to weigh the value of options and think from different perspectives,[1] it is posited that such practice is equally valuable to mediators. Given that a successful mediation is to arrive at an agreement in a situation where both parties have some shared and some opposed interests, it stands to reason that the learning process does not depend on the age of our counterparty.[2]

This chapter aims to explore how negotiation with children can be relevant to us in two aspects. First, from these negotiations, we can learn how to better handle difficult situations, as mediators are bound to face parties who exhibit challenging behaviour similar to children (Section II). Additionally, we can identify certain manipulative, inappropriate or inefficient negotiation techniques adopted by one or both parties and guide them toward better dispute resolution. Second, we can learn the skills which children use when negotiating with us and apply them to our own interactions with parties to a mediation (Section III). It is to be clarified that the purpose of this chapter is not to elucidate new mediation techniques. Rather, it hopes to convince that the exercise of negotiating with children has, and will, sharpen our competence in mediation.

II. How to be better mediators

This section is developed according to the framework of 7 Elements of Negotiation, which has become the backbone of principled negotiation, as espoused in the seminal book by Roger Fisher, *Getting to Yes*.[3] Categorising various interactions into elements of the framework will also provide structure to the following examples which may initially appear amorphous. Although most situations involve children until the age of 8, some of the examples can similarly extend to teenage children.

A. *Interests*

Proposed options should promote mutual gain. It can however, be difficult for mediators to identify the parties' interests, especially when they are not forthcoming in sharing. Given that children start requesting for things as young as two, negotiating with them may have actually given us constant practice in trying to understand a person's interest.[4]

(1) *Ask questions*

Asking children questions is second-nature to us because we know that they struggle to articulate their feelings. Hence, we take the initiative to ask, "Why are you sad?" or "Why do you not want to wear your shoes?" However, this inability to articulate is as relevant to adults, whose interests can likewise be intangible.[5] Asking "why" helps us understand what is important to the parties.[6] With people who do not want to disclose their interests, asking "why not" could indirectly achieve the same effect because people who are reluctant to share their concerns may instead be willing to critique. By getting them to comment on our approach, we obtain valuable information on what their concerns could be.[7] Therefore, if we ask, "Why not do it this way?" and the person replies, "That's a terrible idea! I have two jobs and I have children to take care of", we would have received the information we needed. We can even occasionally disguise questions as statements, so as to prevent the dialogue from appearing interrogatory.[8]

   If one party still remains silent, we can offer what we think their interests are. Children may be unwilling to be the first to divulge information, but they can nonetheless be tempted to correct someone's misunderstanding of their interests. From personal experience of teaching young children from 3 to 8 years old, gently asking sullen children questions such as, "Are you sad because this question is too difficult?" is usually more effective than, "What happened?"[9] The former question may prompt a child to reply that it was not because of the work but because he is hungry, while the latter may generate no response. This instinctive urge to remedy others' misunderstanding of our reasons or emotions is just as strong in adults. Hence, it has been proposed that for reticent adults, we can similarly bring their interests up and ask them to correct us.[10] This approach aims to encourage responses by making proposals of our own, therefore one should not appear accusatory or presumptuous. The intention is not to get the targeted party to agree to our suggestion, but to trigger a reaction and acquire information.

(2) *Do not let one party negotiate around the other*

Negotiating *around* someone is different from negotiating *with* someone. Children commonly negotiate around adults when they want their way. A teenager might persist in wanting to have a friend over by protesting, "You said I shouldn't sit around the house doing nothing." If the parent replies that she is tired, he might retort, "So if you're tired, I can't socialise?" By ignoring the parent's needs, the child is exhibiting the behaviour of negotiating around the parent.[11] In reality, the parent says, "Yes," not because she sees value in the proposal but because she is tired of arguing.

Likewise, it is important to realise when one party is attempting to work around the other person, rather than with him or her. In some instances, he may be using hard bargaining tactics, such as making personal insults or belittling alternatives.[12] When such behaviour is spotted, the mediator should step in and encourage the parties to consider if they are giving each other room to genuinely discuss their interests and options.

(3) *Do not make important decisions on the spot*

Some parents advise against making important decisions on the spot as it will be difficult to change their answer later.[13] Changing from "no" to "yes" may lead the child to think that what he did in the interim, such as crying, was useful while changing from "yes" to "no" may cause the parent to break a promise. To prevent both situations, the parent should tell the child honestly that he or she needs some time to think and that they will answer by the end of the day.

As mediators, it may be important to prevent tricks from parties who attempt to sneak in proposals at the close of discussions. When one party says, "I assume this is included," the mediator should be alert to the possibility that the other party says "yes" on the spot just because of the pressure. In such cases, mediators should encourage parties to have more time to consider the proposal or engage in another round of mediation.[14] Otherwise, one party risks undermining a fair treatment of his or her interests by feeling pressured to agree on the spot and later, have the agreement held against him or her.

B. *Options*

Generating a variety of possibilities before deciding on the solution is crucial to any mediation and negotiating with children may in fact hone our skills in this department. It is for this reason that when interviewed by Stanford University on negotiation lessons learned from his children, Steve Young, a former professional American footballer, reflected that, "Kids have a way of forcing you to slow down and figure out a creative way to not make it about yourself."[15]

(1) *Do not be fixated with the goal and the route which we think is the fastest to get there*

Most parents agree having a well-prepared plan to reach the goal is good, but not fool-proof. Children will inadvertently cause these plans to go awry. In the aforementioned interview, Young applied this to negotiations, reflecting that one should be open to different options of reaching the same goal.[16] Sometimes, we are so focused on the end point of the mediation that we want to get there in the most direct manner. However, we are probably not arriving at the supermarket with young children by driving straight to the store. The kids may instead be distracted; they want a detour for ice-cream; or they want to ride their scooters there. We invariably end up negotiating with the children on how to reach there.

In the same vein, rather than restricting ourselves to one fixed option, one should be open to the fact that in mediations, we almost always need to navigate many times and in different ways to reach the goal.[17] Be open to the possibilities of exploring options and we may invent one which we would not have thought of before had we kept our eyes solely on the goal. Having more options also means more chances of finding a solution which meets both parties' interests.[18]

(2) *Invite the parties into generating options*

Additionally, it is ineffective if parties arrive at the goal with only one of them, or just the mediator, pushing the process. For example, rather than scolding the child who consistently oversleeps in the mornings, one can discuss with him on what to do and the child may suggest buying an alarm clock.[19] When he participates in this decision-making, and later chooses the clock with a design he likes, he is more likely to feel involved and be invested in the solution. Similarly, we can also invite parties in generating options with us. This increases the sense of joint ownership over the ideas and may motivate them to reach an agreement more quickly. Thus, it has been said that while a salesman typically throws out a few options for the customer to choose one, it may be better if the customer is allowed to build on the solutions she offered and jointly work with the salesman for improved options.[20]

C. *Communication*

It seems trite to point out that in mediations, we are interacting with parties who are not us. However, it is important to remember this because communication is not easy even for people who have an enormous background of shared experiences.[21] Thinking about the way we communicate with children, with whom we cannot be more different, will force us to evaluate the methods in which we convey and correspond our ideas.

(1) *Use short sentences*

We know long preambles do not work with children. This is why we break our sentences down into simple ones and speaking succinctly is a skill we employ instinctively when communicating with children. Yet, this technique is recommended for mediations too. A mediator should speak clearly to promote understanding. The longer the statement, the greater the chance of misinterpretation. Thus, one can avoid the risk by breaking complex messages into small parts and allowing pauses so that the listening party can digest the information.[22]

(2) *Do not trivialise the parties' problems; acknowledge them*

Acknowledge their emotions: When a child reacts strongly in some way, telling the child, "Now you are sad and angry, and I understand that, but…" is going to be more effective than saying dismissively, "This is nothing to get angry over."[23] Similarly, we should not gloss over any party's positions by thinking that they are insignificant. Just as we acknowledge the child's fears and insecurities, we do not ignore the adults' emotions. Instead, we should work on breaking through the barriers in order to reach cooperation on both sides.[24] Acknowledging the parties' feelings can be powerful, especially since he or she feels the lack thereof from the other party.

Apology: One powerful form of acknowledgment of the other person's feelings is an apology. A lesson we learn as children is that if we say, "I'm sorry", our parents will not be angry anymore. This is something we either forget or unlearn as we grow up. There is an example of a Columbia law professor whose 8 year old son sat in his class because he could not find a babysitter. When the professor asked the contract class what the seller should do after having defaulted on delivery and the buyer stopped payment, his son spoke up, "I would say I'm sorry."[25] A classic contractual discussion on damages turns out to be a valuable negotiation lesson.

Thus, as mediators, it is useful to identify situations to encourage apologies from the parties. Even if one side is primarily responsible for the situation, the other can consider apologising for his or her share. This can be seen as taking responsibility for their emotions and their apology may bring a corresponding acceptance of responsibility from the other side, allowing parties to resume a working relationship.[26] However, an apology should be sincere. A child who mutters the apology under his breath is likely to be dismissed by the adult. Similarly, one quality of an effective apology is that it should be the result of some analysis and introspection. If it comes off too spontaneously, it loses power and legitimacy.[27]

D. *Relationship*

Humans react, and the instinctive thing to do when faced with a difficult situation is to act without thinking.[28] However, as a quote from Ambrose Bierce goes, "Speak when you are angry and you will make the best speech you will ever regret."[29] Sometimes, it may be better to stop the mediation temporarily in order for the relationship between both parties to resume its functional state.

Children throw tantrums because they think this is how they can get what they want. In response, some parents utilise the "1-2-3" technique, which is a form of time-out. This advocates the stopping of negotiation with children, which may be surprising given the theme of this chapter. However, this may be needed when the child simply has no interest in listening to any constructive arguments. In such situations, say firmly, "That's one," when the child whines. If he persists, say, "That's two". The final warning comes, "That's three," and you bring the child out of the room for a five-minute break.[30] The point of this is to remove emotions from the discipline. Usually, the child returns with a glare but the fury has subsided and he is more likely to listen.

This removal of emotions is vital in situations when to continue mediating is to create more conflict. In this scenario, a time-out is needed. It has been said that the easiest technique to minimise the impact of strong emotions is to interrupt the encounter for a short break.[31] One way to achieve this is to suggest a coffee break.[32] This removes negative emotions, and also provides opportunities for parties to cool down and recall the possible benefits of and motivations behind working together.

94 *Contemporary Issues in Mediation Volume 4*

III. Techniques from children

A study conducted on preschool children who were presented with hypothetical conflict scenarios showed that 63% of them preferred negotiation as a conflict management strategy.[33] This demonstrates that even children as young as 3 years old are capable of a mature understanding of conflict management.[34] However, most young children are not yet able to translate this understanding into skills.[35] Even when they start negotiating around the age of 6, they may engage in positional rather than principled negotiation.[36] Thus, this section is considerably shorter than the first. It is nonetheless mentioned for completeness and to serve as a reminder that children can be very good at resolving conflicts.

A. *Be creative*

Children are known to be imaginative. Childhood was probably the only period in our life when we were in a different occupation every day or played with dolls that transformed into mermaids.[37] We already know that in mediations, it is important to think creatively to expand the pie.[38] However, we can strengthen this notion by remembering how we were when we were younger. Children do not dismiss their ideas because they are "impractical" or "stupid", at least, not until they grow older and become influenced by peers and society. In Fisher's words, judgement hinders imagination.[39] This is perhaps why imagination is said to be the underlying reason for children's special negotiating powers.[40]

B. *Be direct (in appropriate situations)*

Young children are very direct, so a child often says, "I want this."[41] Adults are less straightforward, knowing that being too direct offends people and comes across as rude. However, clarity is important and sometimes, a mediator revealing his or her opinion or recommendation in a round-about manner is ineffective. The chance of mediation serving the parties' interests increases with direct communication.[42] The mediator can also encourage parties to be direct with each other, as the more openly they communicate, the less basis there is for suspicion and misunderstandings.[43] The husband is thus better off being truthful that he does not want to eat out because he is on a diet than saying that he does not like the service of the restaurant which the wife has suggested.

C. *Play the repeat game*

Children like to repeat other people's words to irritate. We must have had at least one experience with a child who echoes our words, "Stop doing that!" Although this is typical childish behaviour, such parroting exercise is something we can actually replicate in mediations.[44]

However, our aim of repeating is not to annoy, but to reassure. This is because repeating parts of what the other person has said can show there is a common vision, which can be helpful in moving stalled mediations forward. If two parties are negotiating over profit-sharing of a business, we can repeat that the partner taking the bigger risk should receive a larger share, even as we disagree on how this risk should be calculated.[45] Stressing the shared interests of both parties can also make the mediation smoother and more amicable.[46] At the very least, repeating the other person's words can be a good way to summarise what we have heard to assure the other party that we have been listening.

IV. Conclusion

Even as adults, we are emotional beings. Thus, negotiating with children is a good reflection of interactions which involve heightened feelings and difficult parties. Since most negotiations with young children involve short-term goals with little emphasis on developing viable alternatives, the scope of this chapter is intentionally limited to interests, options, communication and relationships, leaving out legitimacy, commitment and alternatives.

Just as we ask a child, "What have you learnt today?", setting aside time at the end of mediation is useful to reflect on lessons learned and applying them in future.[47] Perhaps, the most valuable lesson we can draw from children is that they never give up. When they fail at one negotiation, they simply return with another. Similarly, when we face a challenging mediation, we can only improve by being unfazed and constantly honing our skills. At the end of the day, becoming a better mediator is a process, and we can enhance this by learning from those who are in the youngest and freshest phase of their lives.

Learning from Crises:
How Crisis Negotiation Skills
Can Help Mediators Deal with
Parties in Mediation

Ang Wen Qi Therese

I. Introduction

> A meeting over the direction of a startup is going badly. A team member refuses to buy into the vision that the management has crafted, and it seems that the dispute will not be resolved. Just then, the CEO steps in. In a shift that seems almost magical, the member comes around and fully supports the new vision. I ask the CEO what he did, and he replies, "It's something I read about in a book by an FBI hostage negotiator."[1]

Clearly, there is something to be learnt from crisis negotiators. Is their approach any different from the traditional interest-based approach? What makes their approach work?

This chapter puts forth that crisis negotiation techniques can help mediators better deal with emotional or difficult parties, because such techniques have a focus on helping one connect to, manage and mould his counterparty's emotions so that the latter can be influenced into behaving collaboratively (Part III). This chapter then delves into several crisis negotiation techniques mediators can use to better facilitate the resolution of disputes (Part IV).

II. Scope

The interest-based approach has its genesis in negotiation theory; in fact, interest-based mediation has been described as facilitated negotiation.[2] Accordingly, dispute-resolution skills used in interest-based negotiation can be applied effectively in mediation. This is especially so with regard to crisis negotiation techniques — which focus on using people's emotions as a platform for influencing them into behaving collaboratively — because the vast majority of cases brought to mediation have a significant emotional component.[3] Consequently, this chapter aims to explore how crisis negotiation techniques can be used to help mediators manage and influence emotional or difficult parties within the framework of interest-based mediation.

Such techniques will likely typically be used one-on-one between the mediator and the party in question. While this chapter does not elaborate on the principle of neutrality, it is highlighted that in all circumstances, mediators must ensure that the parties know that the process ultimately remains a neutral and non-partisan one.[4] Consequently, even while empathising with and building rapport with the emotional or difficult party, the mediator must ensure that he continues acting in a manner that is seen by *all* parties as neutral and non-partisan.

III. Learning from crisis negotiators — making emotions and relationship-building central to the process

Crisis negotiators deal with a multitude of actors ranging from hostage-takers, barricaded subjects and suicide attempts ("**actor**").[5] These situations usually arise because of unpredictability and a loss of control on the part of the actor.[6] Actors are thus typically driven by heightened negative emotions like anger or fear at the detriment of rational thinking.[7] Because emotions are traditionally perceived as an impediment to reaching resolutions, the assumption is that for a dispute to be resolved, the emotional brain should be overcome by a more rational, joint problem-solving mindset.[8] This is why books like *Getting to Yes* recommend "[separating] the people [(including their emotions)] from the problem".[9]

However, such traditional approaches largely fail to change combative mindsets.[10] This is because we can never truly separate people from their emotions. We are not robots — our emotions inevitably steer our rational thoughts.[11] Therefore, dispute-resolution can never become purely a matter of cool and rational thinking.[12]

Crisis negotiators acknowledge this point in devising their approach. Rather than focussing on *quid-pro-quo* bargaining and problem-solving, emphasis is placed on techniques that not only elicit the verbalisation of interests and build rapport and trust, but also manage and, mould people's emotions instead of taking them out of the picture.[13] All these help the negotiator gain influence over the actor so that the latter may be guided into behaving more collaboratively for a successful resolution.[14] This is why crisis negotiation techniques are effective not only in emotionally driven life-and-death situations, but in any dispute.

IV. Applying crisis negotiation techniques to mediation

A. *Active listening*

As in the traditional interest-based approach, crisis negotiators begin by identifying an actor's specific interests and needs. One technique heavily relied on is active listening; that is, listening and responding to the actor's views and feelings in a manner that shows genuine concern and empathy.[15] By focussing on understanding the actor's situation and validating his emotions, the negotiator makes the actor feel comfortable enough to talk and share more information about himself.[16]

In the same vein, when dealing with a specific party, this skill can be used to help mediators in two ways:

- **Informative:** The mediator can collect vital information about the party's interests and strategies.
- **Affective:** The mediator's demonstration of empathy helps to defuse any negative emotions the party might have. It also builds rapport and trust so that the mediator can subsequently influence a collaborative behavioural change in that party.

(1) *Slowing down the process*

One crucial aspect in active listening is "going slow to go fast". A mediator must invest sufficient time into building a good foundation for his relationship with the party before trying to exert any influence. Trying to speed things up in hopes of facilitating the mediation quickly will make the party feel like he is not actually being heard, thereby diminishing rapport and trust.[17]

Another benefit of "going slow" is that the mediator helps to create a calmer atmosphere by giving the emotional party more time to move from a "hot moment" to a "cool calm".[18] Conversely, if the mediator rushes through the process, this conveys a sense of urgency which escalates rather than defuses negative emotions.[19] The chances of the party being inclined to collaborate with the mediator and his counterparty will accordingly be reduced.

(2) *Micro-skills of active listening*

Crisis negotiators use many micro-skills that mediators can strategically apply to benefit optimally from active listening.

Skill	Description
Open-ended questions/ statements	Open-ended questions or statements can be used to invite a party to open up and share his views.[20] Such questions or statements are especially helpful at the beginning of a mediation to help the mediator clarify what the party has been going through, and to show that party that attention is being paid to him and his feelings.
	A good open-ended statement is non-judgemental, shows interest in the party's story, and is likely to lead to more information about his interests and concerns.[21] One example would be: "Sounds like you had a rough time. Can you tell me your side of the story?". Contrast this with factual questions such as: "Did you supply a defective good?". Similar to questions like, "Do you have a gun?" in crisis negotiations, such factual, close-ended questions only give rise to one-word "yes/no" answers that require little thought. Questions of this type close parties up and diminishes rapport because

(Continued)

Learning from Crises 101

	(*Continued*)
Skill	Description
	they give the impression that the mediator is more interested in assessing the accuracy of the facts rather than in understanding the party's views about the situation.[22]
Effective pauses	The strategic use of silence can be extremely helpful. Mediators can use effective pauses after an open-ended question to allow a party to collect his thoughts and encourage sharing. As crisis negotiators have found, this is particularly important when people are overwhelmed by emotions, because although they may have more to say, they take longer to process their thoughts.[23] Mediators can also use effective pauses after an emotional outburst to defuse heightened feelings of anger, hurt and frustration. By refraining from confronting the party, this prevents negative feelings from escalating and gives that party space to continue ventilating his emotions.[24] Eventually, like a swamp being cleared out, even the most emotionally overwrought people can be calmed down.[25] Mediators must note, however, that if the outburst threatens to disrupt the mediation process — for example, if the other counterparty is significantly affected by the outburst because it was a direct attack against him — then the interest in intervening to protect the neutrality of the process must be duly weighed against that of allowing the emotional party to vent.
Minimal encouragers	Brief, well-timed encouragers can be used to let the party speaking know that the mediator is paying full attention to him and is interested to know more. Good encouragers like "and" and "yes" create room for more explanation without challenging the party, as opposed to "but why?", which would force him to defend his position.[26]

(*Continued*)

102 *Contemporary Issues in Mediation Volume 4*

(*Continued*)

Skill	Description
	Using minimal encouragers is especially helpful if a mediator is seeking to acquire more information because it invites the party to keep talking. It also improves the mediator-party relationship, because it shows that the former is genuinely concerned about the latter's feelings.[27]
Mirroring	Mirroring is a sign that people are in sync and developing the kind of rapport that leads to trust. While this technique is often associated with body language, crisis negotiators focus on mirroring the last few words said by an actor.[28] Whilst seemingly simple, this has proven to be uncannily effective in getting actors to keep talking and reveal damaging admissions, such as the presence of previously unknown accomplices.[29]
	Mediators can use mirroring to facilitate bonding and obtain more information from a party. Not only does this show the party that the mediator is listening to him, it also triggers the former's mirroring instinct to sustain the process of connecting by elaborating on what he just said, potentially revealing interests and concerns that the mediator and the counterparty did not know beforehand.[30]
Paraphrasing	While mirroring is effective, using it too often may give the party the impression that the mediator is merely parroting his concerns. To prevent this, another technique that mediators can use is paraphrasing, whereby the mediator uses his own words to repeat what the party said. Paraphrasing goes one step further from showing that one is listening — it demonstrates that an active effort is being made to understand and connect.
	Encouragers can be used after such paraphrases to invite the party to share more or clarify himself. Such an approach would help mediators gain a fuller and deeper understanding of the situation.[31]

(*Continued*)

Learning from Crises   103

(Continued)

Skill	Description
Emotional labelling	It is hard to "separate people from the problem" when their emotions *are* the problem. Instead of trying to remove emotions from the picture, crisis negotiators aim to identify and understand the feelings of the actor and use this as a means of increasing their ability to influence such actors into behaving more collaboratively.[32] This approach will be extremely useful for mediators when facing emotional parties.

The skill that crisis negotiators use is known as emotional labelling, which is an additive empathetic response that validates someone's emotions by identifying and acknowledging those feelings, rather than judging or minimising them.[33] To begin, the mediator must first detect the emotion driving the party's behaviour and then label it aloud.

- **Detecting feelings**: A lot of information can be gleaned from a person's words, tone and body language. Mediators can detect those feelings by paying close attention to any changes these three areas undergo when the party responds to external events.[34] For example, if the party's voice goes flat when a colleague is mentioned, there could be some animosity between the two.
- **Labelling**: Labels generally start with "*It* seems/sounds/looks like…" instead of "*I'm* hearing that …". The latter will put the party's guard up because it suggests that the mediator is more interested in himself than in the party, and it makes the mediator take personal responsibility for the words used and any offence they might cause.[35] Conversely, when phrased as a neutral statement of understanding, a label encourages the party to be responsive and elaborate on

(Continued)

Skill	Description
	his feelings.[36] Even if he disagrees, the mediator can distance himself from it by saying, "I didn't say that was what it was, I just said it seemed/sounded/looked like that". This prevents the party from feeling like he was being superimposed on and gives him room to clarify his emotions.
	By giving the emotion a name, the mediator shows that he is trying to understand the situation from the party's perspective.[37] This operates as a shortcut to intimacy — it establishes an emotional connection between the mediator and the party without the former having to show bias or agree with the validity of those feelings. Additionally, if the party's negative emotions are high, exposing those feelings to "broad daylight" makes them seem less frightening, thereby defusing them.[38] When people try to label their emotions, brain activity moves from the amygdala (which generates fear) to the areas that govern rational thinking.[39] Labelling an emotion therefore disrupts that emotion's raw intensity and introduces a degree of calmness into the process.
	If utilised well, emotional labelling can further enable mediators to influence a party's consciousness into becoming more collaborative and trusting.[40] By listening to a negative feeling without judgement and replacing it with positive, solution-based thoughts, the mediator induces the party to appreciate the fact that his feelings are being empathised with, and that an effort is being made to help him and his counterparty find a solution.[41] Such displays of tactical empathy are how certain veteran police officers manage to talk angry people out of fights or get them to put down their weapons. These police officers know that if they empathise, they can use those negative emotions as a platform to influence people to become more cooperative.[42]

(Continued)

Skill	Description
Summarising	Summarising is a combination of paraphrasing and labelling: it is rearticulating the meaning of what was said and acknowledging the emotions underlying those meanings.[43] Mediators can use this to let a party know that he has been heard and understood, fortifying the rapport and trust built between them in the process.

The ultimate goal of using all these skills is to get the party to say, "*That's* right."[44] In crisis negotiations, this marks a crucial point where the actor feels heard and acknowledged, showing that a connection has been established between him and the negotiator.[45] It is at this juncture when the negotiator typically gains the actor's "permission" to persuade him, opening the door to exploring previously impossible solutions.[46] The more a person feels understood, the more his urge for collaborative behaviour takes hold.[47] This is because, sometimes, underneath all their substantive demands, parties may actually just want their feelings to be truly heard.

Jeff Schilling's case is an illustrative example. Sabaya, the rebel leader, held Schilling hostage and demanded war damages for the oppression Muslim Filipinos had gone through. No matter how negotiators tried to reason that Schilling had nothing to do with the war damages, Sabaya refused to listen. Then the negotiators changed their approach. They empathised with the group's predicament, used mirroring, encouraging and labelling to soften Sabaya up and begin shifting his perspective and finally, summarised his story and emotions. Sabaya was silent, and then he spoke, "that's right." From then on, the war damages demand disappeared.[48]

B. *Influence techniques*

The techniques below help crisis negotiators disarm and redirect actors in a relationship-affirming way so that conflict is transformed into collaboration, and options that previously seemed impossible can be explored. Because change must come from within the actor, negotiators control this problem-solving process in an indirect way to reduce chances of resistance.[49]

106　*Contemporary Issues in Mediation Volume 4*

Such skills can similarly be applied by mediators to influence an emotional or difficult party into behaving more collaboratively so that the mediation process can be more effectively facilitated.

(1) *Reinforcing movement towards resolution*

Mediators should reinforce any movement in the direction of a successful resolution, such as a party's willingness to cooperate with his counterparty or a resolution of any ambivalence or opposition to an option. This subtly nudges the party to display more collaborative qualities.

Skill	Description
Comments of appreciation	One way crisis negotiators have reinforced desirable movement is by giving clear comments of appreciation on specific actions of actors, such as by thanking them for lowering their weapons.[50] Along these lines, mediators can show appreciation towards a difficult party whenever he displays collaborative behaviour, for instance, when he appears willing to listen to an option suggested by his counterparty. As behaviour that is acknowledged tends to increase, doing so makes it likely that the party will start exhibiting more cooperative behaviour.[51]
Nominalising actions into qualities	Nominalising positive actions of a party into permanent qualities entails a strategic manipulation of language. The mediator must change the verb describing the *action* into an adjective describing an *inherent character trait* in the party.[52]
	For example, where an emotional party has calmed down, the mediator can say, "I appreciate how careful a person you are. You are a calm person who thinks things through." This suggests that rational behaviour is a characteristic of the party that can be expected throughout the process.[53]

(2) *Calibrated questions*

Interest-based problem solving involves coaxing, not overcoming; collaboration, not defeating.[54] Mutual agreements are more likely reached if all parties are involved in the process and come up with solutions themselves.

In crisis negotiations, negotiators achieve this by using calibrated questions to involve the actors: "How can I help to make this better for us?". Calibrated questions should be adapted slightly to suit the mediation context, where the focus is on how the parties, and not the mediator, can meet each other's interests. Mediators could ask questions along the lines of, "What can [*counterparty*] do to help [*meet the interest in question*]?".

By asking these questions, the mediator implicitly asks the party for help, triggering goodwill and lessening defensiveness.[55] More importantly, this gives the party the illusion of control, prompting him to use his mental and emotional resources to overcome challenges and obstacles that his counterparty might be facing in coming up with feasible options. Because calibrated questions do not explicitly point out the problem, the mediator helps to subconsciously educate the party on what the problem between him and his counterparty might be, without creating more conflict.[56]

C. *Finding the "Black Swan"*

In the past, negotiators assumed that hostage-takers would not kill hostages on deadlines because they were needed alive as bargaining chips, until William Griffin became the first actor in the history of the United States to prove this wrong.[57] Negotiation has worked in the past with nationalistic organisations like the Irish Republican Army and even religious militant groups like the Moro Islamic Liberation Front, but this was because those groups had limited political goals that could be negotiated with.[58] In contrast, the Islamic State of Iraq and the Levant (ISIS) has just encouraged its terrorists to take hostages not for the sake of negotiating any demands, but for the sole purpose of killing them.[59]

Every negotiation and mediation is a new experience. We must let what we know guide us, but not blind us to other possible realities. In every dispute, there are likely to be pieces of information that, if discovered, would change everything. Voss, a former Federal Bureau of Investigation (FBI) hostage negotiator, refers to these as "Black Swans". In Griffin's case, he had no orthodox demands and his note to the police included a line, "… after the police take my life …". Because these were not uncovered, the negotiators failed to see this novel situation for what it was: Griffin did not want to negotiate for money or transport, he wanted to be killed.[60]

Such Black Swans certainly also exist in mediation. To uncover them, mediators must always challenge their assumptions, put them out on the table, and listen to the response of the party in question. When a party refuses to agree to a solution that appears to be in his interests, one may assume that he is irrational or difficult to please. But it may actually be that he is simply ill-informed, constrained by promises already made or by a lack of authority, or has hidden interests — emotional, substantive or otherwise — that have not been addressed. Mediators must not let their assumptions shut them off to these possibilities. They must strive to uncover the Black Swans hidden from them and the other party to ensure effective facilitation of the mediation process.

V. Conclusion

Most mediations will likely never be conducted in life-threatening crisis situations. But incorporating the skills explored earlier into one's skillset will undoubtedly help mediators become better at connecting with and managing the emotions of parties, so that such parties can be positively influenced into behaving collaboratively for the effective resolution of any dispute.

Equal but Different?
Exploring How Gender Roles
Shape the Power Balance in
Family-Related Mediation

Lee Kwang Chian

I. Introduction

There is a certain scepticism attached to family-related mediation. Critics of mediation disagree that it is effectual, unless parties are of equal bargaining power.[1] They argue the inherent impossibility of ensuring a fair outcome when there is an imbalance in the power dynamic; indeed, it is not uncommon for feminist advocates to protest that the mediation process unfairly shifts control towards the men, especially in a patriarchal society.[2] And yet, this flies in the face of the traditional mindset regarding mediation. Since the medium of mediation emphasises communication, and reducing acrimony between parties,[3] it would seem to be the perfect medium for resolving familial disputes. After all, unlike ordinary disputes, family-related mediation will involve long term interaction between the parties, especially where children are involved.

This chapter shall briefly discuss the academic discourse regarding the gender-power disparity in Part II, and the arguments for/against allowing mediation in family disputes. This chapter will further consider how local customs and mindsets influence the balance of power between the genders. Part III looks at the schools of thought regarding the issue of power imbalances and considers the approaches that mediators may undertake to resolve issues of power imbalances, and suggests changes to the role of mediators in addressing such power imbalances. It is hoped that this chapter would create an understanding of the sensitive topic of gender-power imbalances in mediation, especially in the Singaporean context.

II. Power imbalance in mediation: Does gender play a part?

A. *Arguments against family-related mediation*

(1) *The nature of the familial relationship*

Power in mediation has been defined as "the ability of a person in a relationship to influence or modify an outcome."[4] Indeed, there is an ever-present belief that mediation allows for stronger parties to impose their will on weaker parties because mediation emphasises the power imbalances and the system does not provide effective checks and balances.[5]

This is especially pertinent in familial disputes, which bring within it an implicit abuse of a prior relationship of trust and confidence. It has been argued that mediated agreements arising from a climate of intimidation or violence would rarely be able to reach an equitable decision.[6] How then could one allow mediation if there has been any history of family violence or power disparity?

It is clear that a significant number of mediators do not find mediation appropriate where there has been a history of familial violence (refer to Table 1 for a detailed breakdown of their responses), or essentially, where there is a chance that the power imbalance between the parties (especially given the coercive nature of many abusive relationships) will permeate the mediation.[7]

Table 1. Mediators' responses to the statement "Mediation is appropriate where there has been a history of domestic violence"[8]

	Strongly Disagree	Disagree	Undecided	Agree	Strongly Agree	Total Disagree	Total Agree
Male	24%	32%	16%	28%	0%	56%	28%
Female	36%	30%	18%	15%	0%	66%	15%
Total	31%	31%	17%	21%	0%	62%	21%

(2) *The traditional status of men/women in Singapore*

Indeed, even in situations where no abuse has occurred, many feminist advocates believe that women should not participate in mediation due to their traditional status as the "weaker" party in society.[9]

In a relatively traditional country like Singapore, women still experience a marked disparity in economic power and information, and the credibility gap between genders still exists. On average, women in Singapore are likely to have lower incomes than men.[10] Furthermore, there is a perennial belief that men should be the breadwinner, ensuring that generally, men would be able to afford to wait out an extended delay in negotiation/mediation, and can raise more issues than their financially-dependent counterparts.[11]

In addition, if a woman is in a weaker financial situation, she may be forced to accept an early settlement and ultimately settle for less than what she is entitled to at law.[12] Women who are "traditionally disempowered or ... oppressed by a particular relationship, negotiate for what they think they can get, rather than what is... equitable."[13] Indeed, agreements reached in mediation on family disputes tend to be less favourable to women than those achieved in the courts.[14]

Finally, there is a credibility gap between the genders in society.[15] Women are more likely to be treated with disbelief, or not taken seriously, and tend to have more features associated with powerlessness than men do.[16]

Indeed, where the mediation proceedings involve an abused spouse, such considerations are even more pertinent. Many critics of mediation contend that where the familial dispute is between an abused party and their abuser, the abused party should not be forced into mediation, as it is impossible that the abused party would be on an equal footing to their abuser.[17] Critics argue that the mere presence of an abusive partner will inevitably ensure that a power imbalance between the parties would exist.[18] Indeed, the inherent psychological fear cannot be erased merely by the promise of "fair" mediation, especially when an abuser may also be subtly intimidating or threatening their spouse with verbal/non-verbal cues. This presents a problem for the mediation process; an abused party must alert the mediator to prior abusive conduct of their abuser, and yet it would take strong mental resilience for the abused party to speak out in front of their abuser.[19]

The end result is that abused spouses would be unlikely to communicate truthfully during the mediation process and would not be able to attain an equitable settlement of the dispute.[20] Furthermore, it is likely that the abused party would acquiesce to the demands of their abuser out of fear for their "physical, psychological or financial" wellbeing.[21] Critics argue that any settlement derived from such a mediation would be wholly unjust, as it would have been formed from the capitulation of the abused party to the whims of their abuser.[22]

(3) *The forward-thinking mindset of mediation*

Mediation is premised on opening up communication channels between parties and decreasing possible hostility between the parties.[23] Mediations are successful precisely because they try to mitigate accusations of prior fault, and instead look towards solving issues arising in the future.

However, it is this aspect of the mediation process that creates issues when dealing with familial disputes, especially where parties have been abused or aggrieved by their spouse.[24] While the intent of forward-thinking mediation is to ensure that parties are able to reach an amicable settlement, it has the subsidiary effect of silencing the aggrieved spouse.[25]

This creates a power imbalance as the prior abuses one spouse has suffered may be seen as being "brushed aside" by the mediator (who has done nothing but emphasised forward-thinking solutions).[26] This is perhaps most succinctly enunciated by a quote from Kathy Mack,[27] "although mediators have responded to feminist critics by expressing concern for domestic violence, their insistence on prospectivity and on avoiding accusations of guilt may have the effect of preventing the issue of violence from surfacing."[28]

B. *Arguments for family-related mediation*

(1) *Promotes communication and creates a collaborative space*

However, even parties who argue that mediation may be unfair for the parties cannot disagree that mediation does create an avenue for communication that was erstwhile closed off to the parties.[29] Indeed, our current Chief Justice of the Singapore Courts, Chief Justice Sundaresh Menon has observed that divorce-related mediation has helped "parents appreciate the consequences of their actions on their children, with encouraging results."[30] It was highlighted that mediation remains one of the most practical options for family-related disputes as it provides estranged families with an avenue of communication that is non-hostile and collaborative in nature.[31]

Indeed, even in cases where familial violence had occurred, many believe that it is still in the best interests of the parties to communicate and talk things through. In fact, a good mediator should be able to reframe issues to help the abuser understand how the abused spouse may feel, while ensuring that the abuser does not feel like he is under attack, and yet allowing the abused party to feel safe.[32]

Furthermore, between the other forms of legal action/dispute resolution, mediation should still be the preferred choice. The adversarial nature of litigation would encourage abusive spouses to entrench themselves and attempt to implicate their victim with various allegations/counterclaims in order to avoid the hostility that would follow.[33] In contrast, mediation allows parties to communicate effectively with one another and behave collaboratively in dealing with their familial issues, especially where both sides feel that they have been fairly treated.[34]

Indeed, there is evidence that couples who chose mediation actually experienced a marked decrease in incidences of familial abuse/violence.[35] Even for cases where familial violence has occurred, it is impossible to generalise the effectiveness (or lack thereof) of mediation. Mediation should not be automatically removed as an option merely due to the fear of a possible power imbalance between parties.

In fact, most mediators would agree that mediation is still an appropriate forum of dispute resolution (even if spousal abuse has occurred) as long as parties make an informed choice to participate in the mediation process (refer to Table 2). Even for situations where familial abuse has been identified, it is submitted that the option of mediation should ultimately rest in the hands of the abused party. In this regard, an opt in or opt out procedure is preferred.

Table 2. Mediators' responses to the statement "Mediation is appropriate if a victim of violence makes an informed decision to participate"[36]

	Strongly Disagree	Disagree	Undecided	Agree	Strongly Agree	Total Disagree	Total Agree
Male	4%	8%	20%	52%	16%	12%	68%
Female	6%	12%	21%	48%	9%	18%	57%
Total	5%	10%	21%	50%	12%	15%	62%

(2) *Parties should be given as much autonomy as required*

In support, scholars argue that an abused spouse should be given the opportunity to engage in mediation if he or she wants to do so, provided the relevant safeguards are in place.[37] The abused party knows his or her situation best, so it would be foolish to force a blanket removal of the right to mediation. However, this right must be contingent on the ability of the mediator to accurately detect and prevent coercion stemming from a power imbalance between the parties.

It is up to the mediator's ability to help parties generate options that can be advantageous to both parties and anticipate scenarios where a lower-power party might be coerced or intimidated into a settlement. In ensuring that mediation can still occur with victims of spousal abuse, a mediator must be prepared to unilaterally "terminate negotiations rather than permit an uninformed or intimidated party to agree to a settlement that may be unrealistic or unfair."[38]

(3) *Safeguards are already in place*

Furthermore, safeguards are in place to ensure that parties are not subject to a power imbalance. The Singapore Mediation Centre has a conscious policy to match a male and female mediator[39] specifically to ensure that the process is free from such gender-bias perception. Indeed, Deputy Executive Director of the Singapore Mediation Centre, Ms. Sabiha Shiraz, has stated that the purpose of the male-female pairings in such familial disputes is due to the inherent difference in gender perceptions, and the requirements that gender-based mediation is not only fair, but appears fair to both parties of the dispute.[40]

III. Gender imbalance: Schools of thought

Given that mediation is still an important tool for family-related disputes, this chapter shall consider several proposed solutions to the issue of power imbalances during mediation. The application of mediation in situations of gender-based power imbalances will need to be thoroughly considered and reviewed.

A. *Leaving it be?*

Many authors have submitted that equal power is not necessary for a mediation to be fair.[41] Indeed, it must be noted that overwriting traditional gender-normative roles held by the parties merely to create fairness in mediation is undesirable for all parties. It is claimed that equal power in fact reduces the possibility of successful mediation because "symmetry in conflict situations tends to produce and reinforce hostility and prolong negotiations."[42] Counterintuitively, equal power creates a situation where parties do not wish to collaborate.[43] This is detrimental for families with young children, as the well-being of their children should be their primary concern.

Furthermore, it is argued that even though most relationships tend to have a large power imbalance favouring one party, it does not mean that that party is able or willing to abuse their power. Indeed, a "disproportionately greater power on the part of one party in a negotiation often reduces the likelihood of a favourable outcome for the power party."[44] Since parties attend mediation in the hopes of attaining some form of resolution, it is unlikely that a party with more power would be able to dictate proceedings without substantial pushback from their partner.[45]

However, the power imbalance, especially in familial/gender disputes, should not be wholly ignored merely for the sake of expediency. It is noted that women's decisions during familial mediations tend to be informed by their "role as nurturers and caretakers, and not as self-interested autonomous individuals."[46] Women are more likely to allow their own interests to be jeopardised in the mediation process, as they have a tendency to value the sanctity of their familial relationship (and the needs of their children), as opposed to their own potential needs and wants.[47]

B. *Embracing the power disparity*

An alternative method would be to embrace the power disparity and allow the mediator to actually discuss and negotiate on the basis that there is an inherent disparity in power (as opposed to the forward-thinking approach). It is suggested that instead of ignoring the power divide between the parties, mediators "who openly discuss sources of power will be more

116   *Contemporary Issues in Mediation Volume 4*

successful in educating disputants and assisting with constructive decision making."[48]

Indeed, in a traditionally patriarchal society like Singapore, it is important to note that while it is inappropriate to allow for a gender-based power disparity to affect the mediation, it is similarly unwise to pretend that symmetrical power dynamics are possible in Singaporean culture.[49]

The traditional dynamic in Singapore gives rise to Confucian values,[50] such as a wife being subservient to her husband. Therefore, a mediator must be able to note these inherent values when attempting to mediate between couples or spouses. Concerns about his "face" may lead a husband to demand more concessions than he should reasonably expect, in order to preserve his "position" as head of the household, and not be seen as an inferior party.[51] Conversely, the wife in the mediation may feel a need to give in to her husband's demand, out of a belief that she must be subservient, or due to her wish to preserve the dignity of her husband.[52]

Instead of attempting to skirt these issues through the forward-thinking approach, it is better for the mediator to address such issues and seek to balance the need to save "face" for each party, with the actual needs of both parties. To do so, he would have to navigate the highly context-based Singaporean culture (which then has implications on how to handle the situation, and which communication styles should be espoused).[53] Mediation styles that would protect the "face" of the parties would create cooperation with the mediation process, while a confrontational or assertive mediator might create the opposite effect, causing the party with more power to feel targeted (and shamed), making the party unlikely to cooperate with the process.

C. *Levelling the playing field*

Having regard to the inherent issues of the gender-power imbalance, it is submitted that there is no real method to level the playing field, and ensure a symmetrical power dynamic.[54] However, mediators should not merely turn a blind eye to such situations. It is submitted that the proper approach is for mediators to approach family-related mediation with the knowledge that there is a gender-power imbalance, and tread carefully in ensuring that such imbalances do not contribute to unfairness in the mediation process. Instead, mediation should allow such parties to have a collaborative space, to iron out their disagreements and to reduce the chance of hostility.[55]

IV. Conclusion

The trickiest aspect of mediation is that no consensus exists as to the best way to mediate a situation; balancing the power imbalance in family-related mediation is a difficult task. Indeed, it goes to the root of traditional gender roles, and the role that a mediator should play in such situations. No clear answer presents itself, and yet it is important that the status quo should not remain.

The inherent power imbalance between genders, especially in traditional Asian societies, is a pertinent issue that must be solved, given that Singapore has already made mediation mandatory for specific types of familial disputes.[56] With a more intimate understanding of the issue, it is hoped that Singapore's mediators can proceed to create a more comprehensive mediation framework that would seek to address such considerations for future family-related mediations.

Are All Expressions of Anger Equal or Are Some More Equal Than Others?

Wesley Aw Ming Xuan

I. Introduction

United States Senator Howard Baker, also known as the "Great Conciliator", once said, "The most difficult thing in any negotiation, almost, is making sure that you strip it of the emotion and deal with the facts." Similarly, in *Getting to Yes*, the authors emphasised the importance of separating the people from the problem and how a good negotiator should not be taunted into reacting with emotions.[1] Emotions have the tendency to drive people to take up positions, clouding their vision of the real interests underlying a mediation and can potentially jeopardise the success of the mediation. Some mediators even consider emotions to be irrelevant because it only escalates tension and derails productive discussion.[2] Yet, current mediation research encourages drawing out such emotions from mediating parties because it can uncover underlying issues and lead to better mediated outcomes.[3] Nevertheless, research has shown that not all parties can use anger with equal effect. This chapter thus seeks to identify how anger can affect a party personally (intrapersonally) and how anger can affect his counterparty (interpersonally). This chapter also seeks to show how the effects of anger both intrapersonally and interpersonally are unequal and vary according to a party's circumstances. This would help mediators to better be able to decide whether anger should have a role to play at the mediation table and whether mediators should take a proactive role in eliciting emotions from parties.

II. Intrapersonal effects of anger during mediation

Anger can be defined as "an emotion that involves an appraisal of responsibility for wrongdoing by another person or entity and often includes the goal of correcting the perceived wrong".[4] Indeed, anger appears to have no place in mediation if the objective of the mediation is simply to achieve an agreement on certain issues. The fault-based attitude underlying anger may appear to be irrational and unreasonable[5] as it risks eliciting reciprocal anger and stalling the mediation.[6] Furthermore, anger causes people to think less clearly and may cause parties to neglect their real interests and goals.[7]

Nevertheless, one study by Tsai and Young (2010) showed that anger can reduce the effect of confirmation bias (i.e. the cognitive tendency to favour information that confirms our pre-existing beliefs).[8] Consequently, anger can cause parties to become more open-minded than parties who do not express their anger or suppress their anger. Although an angry party may be antagonistic and defensive, he would also be in a detail-oriented state of mind in order to rebut errors or inconsistencies.[9]

This is consistent with a study conducted by Overbeck *et al.* (2010) which found that anger can help powerful negotiators become more cognitively focussed and behaviourally tough. However, the same effect was not found when low-power negotiators expressed anger.[10] Angry low-power negotiators showed less apparent cooperativeness and were in less control of their emotions compared to high-power negotiators.[11] It is thus apparent that not all displays of anger have equal intrapersonal effects. A mediator should thus distinguish between high-power parties and low-power parties and determine whether allowing them to vent their anger at the mediation table would be productive in resolving the issue at hand.

Nevertheless, research has shown that the expression of emotion can help parties better understand themselves.[12] Mediators who encourage parties to talk about their emotions help these parties better understand what they feel and why they feel that way. It also helps to integrate their thoughts and feelings, giving them a greater sense of control of the situation.[13] If this is the case, mediators should encourage all parties to talk about their emotions to help both the mediator and the party in question better understand the situation and the underlying interests of the party, especially during private caucuses.

III. Interpersonal effects of anger during mediation

Although allowing a party to express anger may benefit him intrapersonally by allowing him to surface underlying tensions, issues and problems, that expression of anger would also have an effect on his counterparty's cognitive state. This section highlights some of the factors that mediators should take into account when considering whether allowing an expression of anger during a mediation where both parties are present would be useful in moving the mediation forward.

A. *Power balance*

Five types of bases for power have been identified and studied by negotiation scholars: coercive power, reward power, expert power, legitimate power and referent power.[14] Coercive power refers to the ability to punish a counterparty for undesired behaviour while reward power refers to the ability to reward a counterparty for desired behaviour. Expert power comes from a person's experience, knowledge or expertise in a field. Legitimate power refers to a counterparty's belief that a negotiator has a legitimate right to dictate or determine how one should behave while referent power is based on a counterparty's admiration of the negotiator. These five bases are useful starting points for mediators to determine how much power the mediating parties wield in relation to each other.

It was found that anger has a relatively low influence when used against a high-power counterparty. In comparison, anger when used against a low-power counterparty was effective as such counterparties appear to be more sensitive to displays of emotion.[15] This could be attributed to the fact that parties wielding greater power in a mediation tend to be able to conduct themselves freely without much concern of the potential consequences, unlike a low-power party who may be heavily dependent on the high-power party.

Awareness of the difference in power can often be abused by the high-power party. Studies have shown that high-power parties can strategically use anger to extract larger concessions from their counterparties,[16] especially if such high-power party is aware that their counterparties have an underlying motivation or need to consider the high-power party's emotions.[17] Furthermore, anger can cause the low-power party to make fewer demands and larger concessions as compared to a high-power party who sends happy messages.[18] This is because anger is often associated with tough negotiators who adopt a "take it or leave it" stance in the negotiation. Anger would thus indicate to a low-power party that a proposed term or option is unacceptable and falls outside the limits of what the angry party is willing to accept. In contrast, a high-power party who tries to adopt a rational approach that is devoid of any expression of emotions would not be able to achieve the same concessions.[19] A low-power party with weak alternatives would thus have to concede to the terms proposed by the angry high-power party in order to reach an outcome that is better than an impasse.[20] It also suggests that negative consequences (such as an impasse) may follow if the anger recipient insists on pursuing his stance.[21]

In contrast, if the low-power party has viable alternatives, the power dynamics between the two parties would change significantly. This is especially stark in the case of multiparty negotiations and mediations that depends on coalition formation.[22] In such a scenario, weaker parties will always have the option of forming a coalition to the exclusion of an angry party. Here, anger would be an ineffective strategy, even if used by a stronger party. Similarly, in the case of a bilateral dyadic mediation, if the non-angry party has the power and ability to walk away from the mediation, he would most certainly do so, leaving the angry party with none of the benefits of expressing anger.[23]

The results from the research on the interaction between power and anger seem to cohere with real-life situations. For example, in a dispute between an employee and an employer, the employee is unlikely to succeed even if he resorts to anger against an employer given the power dynamics between the two parties. However, the power balance can sometimes be in favour of an employee if he has special expertise knowledge that is valuable to the company or if he had had access to trade secrets of the company. Mediators should thus be sensitive to the power balance between the parties in order to determine whether allowing expressions of anger may help to move the mediation forward. In addition, mediators should also pay attention to possible strategic manipulation by high-power parties and encourage low-power parties to objectively consider the situation such that concessions are not made which the low-power party may subsequently regret. Otherwise, the mediated settlement would merely be a temporary stopgap measure instead of a successful resolution of the dispute.

B. *Culture*

Without a doubt, culture plays a role in the styles that a mediating party tends to adopt.[24] Apart from the effects that it has on one's personal negotiation style, culture also has an effect on the way parties react and respond to anger. For example, in a study conducted by Adam, it was found that European American negotiators made greater concessions compared to Asian or Asian American negotiators when both groups of negotiators faced an angry counterparty.[25] Another study by Kopelman found that East Asian negotiators were less likely to accept offers made by angry counterparties as opposed to Israeli negotiators.[26]

The difference in responses to anger based on culture was attributed to how anger was perceived in different cultural contexts. Adam noted that anger was more acceptable amongst European Americans, and less appropriate amongst Asians. Similarly, Kopelman noted that Israelis had a culture of *dugri*, or speaking about things directly and straightforwardly rather than to beat around the bush. The cultural acceptance of anger and bluntness in non-East Asian cultures results in anger having less of a negative effect on the outcome of the negotiation.

Conversely, "face" plays an important role in East Asian cultures, creating an expectation of respect, which includes humility and deference.[27] The concept of "face" also leads East Asians to avoid and dislike direct confrontation. Furthermore, Asian cultures tend to be more collectivist, compared to Western cultures which are more individualistic.[28] An expression of anger may thus be interpreted as hostility and an intention to be adversarial in future relationships. It also implies that the person who expressed anger will only be self-interested even in future dealings. This is contrary to the collectivist attitude that is built upon mutual trust and respect. In the face of an angry counterparty, it would thus not be unusual for an Asian negotiator to be averse to reaching an agreement if he finds that the anger was unjustified. This conclusion is consistent with the results in Liu's study, which found that Chinese participants tended towards a more competitive approach which focused on claiming value for themselves when their counterparty employed anger during negotiations.[29] Allowing a party to express anger in the presence of his counterparty where cultural factors play a significant role may thus stall the mediation process.[30] Mediators should thus be aware of any cultural differences that exist between parties and how parties subconsciously perceive and react to anger.

C. *Long-term effects of employing anger*

The expression of anger in a mediation has implications beyond the duration of the mediation itself, especially if the concluded mediation agreement contemplates a future relationship between the two parties. Assuming that the two parties continue to engage with each other, there are broadly two possible outcomes when a party meets the same angry counterparty again. Van Kleef termed the two possibilities the spillover hypothesis and the retaliation hypothesis.[31] Under the spillover hypothesis, the party who conceded to an angry counterparty in an earlier negotiation would demand less and make similar concessions because the angry counterparty is perceived to be a tough negotiator. Under the retaliation hypothesis, the conceding party would demand more, as he would be motivated by feelings of resentment towards the angry counterparty, coupled with an intention to get even.

Van Kleef's study found support for the spillover hypothesis and limited support for the retaliation hypothesis.[32] Expressions of anger will instill negative impressions and reduce the likelihood of a future relationship especially if a party has the liberty to choose his or her counterparties.[33] However, in the absence of such choice, it has been found that a negotiator would likely place lower demands against a counterparty who has previously expressed anger.[34] Van Kleef further found that apologising after expressing anger can mitigate the negative consequences of anger.[35]

Van Kleef's study, taken on its own, suggests that anger can have a positive effect for parties who choose to employ it in the long run. However, a subsequent study by Wang found that despite an *overt* concession when a counterparty expresses anger, the recipient of anger would engage in *covert* retaliatory behaviour, such as denying gratifying opportunities or imposing significant obstacles for the angry party after a negotiation.[36] Such covert retaliatory behaviour occurred regardless of whether the recipient of anger was a high-power or a low-power party.[37] This is significant as the benefits or concessions obtained overtly during the mediation may be defeated by covert action taken by the party who feels like he has not been treated fairly during the mediation process. This would defeat the purpose of the mediation since parties would simply return to more adversarial forms of dispute resolution to resolve their dispute in the long run. Mediators should thus also consider the effects of anger on any possible long-term relationship on the parties, and to also get parties to consider how bringing their anger to the mediation table can be counterproductive to arriving at a mediated agreement.

D. *Faking anger*

It would not be surprising to find parties who strategically use anger to try to intimidate or gain an advantage over their counterparties in a negotiation.[38] However, studies have shown that anger that is perceived as fake may backfire, causing counterparties to concede less than if the negotiator had displayed genuine anger or did not display any anger at all.[39] Inauthentic anger or surface acted anger was defined to be displaying anger that is not genuinely felt, creating a mismatch between the internal emotional state and the external perceivable emotional state. Interestingly, negotiators whose anger appeared inauthentic and those whose anger appeared authentic both created an impression of toughness.[40] Instead, the difference in responses against both displays of anger was attributed to the degree of trust that the recipient of the anger could place on the angry party. Inauthentic anger resulted in less favourable results because the recipient perceives the inauthentically angry party to be less trustworthy.[41]

A party who consciously attempts to employ anger during a mediation in order to achieve a strategic goal is likely to be sufficiently rational and in control of himself. The tension between what that party thinks he should feel, what he really feels and what he is perceived to feel from a third-party perspective may send conflicting signals to his counterparty. This internal conflict can create an impression of inauthentic anger. Additionally, the mixed signals may make it difficult for the counterparty to see the angry negotiator as trustworthy. If a mediator finds himself questioning the authenticity of a party's display of anger, he or she might want to consider calling for a caucus to understand the intentions of that party and explain how such a charade may be counterproductive to the mediation.

IV. Final thoughts

This chapter has attempted to give a broad overview of how expressions of anger during a mediation can affect parties intrapersonally and inter-personally. It is clear that not all expressions of anger are equal. Nevertheless, it is possible to predict how an expression of anger can affect a party and his counterparty based on circumstances such as the power balance between the parties, the cultural backgrounds of the parties and the genuineness of the expression of anger. High-power parties appear to be able to wield anger to their advantage and may even do so intentionally. Yet if such anger appears inauthentic, it may cause the anger recipient to be less trusting of the anger user. This may affect the ability of the mediating parties to reach any agreement. Even if an agreement is put on paper, the anger user may be subject to covert retaliatory acts after the mediation by the party who feels like he was unfairly treated. Nevertheless, such consequences of expressing anger may not be as acute in a Western context, as compared to an Asian one.

While it is true that mediators can elicit emotions from parties to move the mediation forward, this chapter hopefully shows that the circumstances of the parties can also play a role in the effectiveness of eliciting such emotions. In general, it is likely to be effective to elicit emotions of anger during private caucuses but mediators should take into account the aforementioned factors if they are considering to elicit emotions during the joint mediation sessions.

End Notes

Chapter 1 What's in a Nudge? How Choice Architecture Surrounding Dispute Resolution Options Can Increase Uptake of Mediation

1. While mediation has always been present in some form in Asian culture, one starting point for institutionalised mediation could be then Attorney-General Chan Sek Keong's speech at the Opening of the Legal Year 1996 on the need to look into mediation as a form of alternative dispute resolution and suggestion to establish a commercial mediation centre.

2. Tan Tam Mei, "Singapore Mediation Centre saw record number of cases and disputed sums in 2017", *The Straits Times* (16 January 2018) <http://www.straitstimes.com/singapore/singapore-mediation-centre-saw-record-number-of-cases-and-disputed-sums-in-2017> (accessed 6 April 2018).

3. The figures are 71% for arbitration and 24% for litigation. Singapore Academy of Law International Promotion of Singapore Law Committee, "Study on Governing Law & Jurisdictional Choices in Cross-Border Transactions" (11 January 2016) at Section 3; Nadja Alexander, "Nudging Users Towards Cross-Border Mediation: Is It Really About Harmonised Enforcement Regulation?" (2014) 7(2) *Contemporary Asia Arbitration Journal* 405 (*"Nadja"*) at 408.

4. *Nadja*, see above note 3; Thomas S. Ulen, "The Importance of Behavioral Law" in Eyal Zamir & Doron Teichman, eds., *The Oxford Handbook of Behavioral Economics and the Law* (Oxford University Press, 2015).

5. Richard H. Thaler, Cass R. Sustein & John P. Balz, "Choice Architecture" in Eldar Shafir, ed., *The Behavioral Foundations of Public Policy* (Princeton University Press, 2012) (*"Thaler et al."*).

6. *Nadja*, see above note 3 at 412; Cass R. Sunstein, "The Ethics of Nudging" (2015) 32(2) *Yale Journal on Regulation* 413 at 420 to 422.

7. Nadja Alexander, "Nudging Cross-border Mediation Forward", *Kluwer Mediation Blog* (April 2014) <http://mediationblog.kluwerarbitration.com/2014/04/14/nudging-cross-border-mediation-forward/> (accessed 6 April 2018).

8. Cass R. Sunstein, "Deciding by Default" (2013) 162(1) *University of Pennsylvania Law Review* 1 ("*Cass*") at 17 to 20; Cass R. Sunstein, "Behavioral Analysis of Law" (1997) 64(4) *The University of Chicago Law Review* 1175 ("*Sunstein*") at 1179 to 1181.

9. *Cass*, see above note 8 at 20 to 21.

10. *Cass*, see above note 8 at 21 to 23.

11. *Sunstein*, see above note 8 at 1182 to 1184; Cass R. Sunstein, "The Storrs Lectures: Behavioral Economics and Paternalism" (2013) 122(7) *The Yale Law Journal* 1826 ("*Storrs Lectures*") at 1848 to 1851.

12. *Sunstein*, see above note 8 at 1183; Linda Babcock and George Loewenstein, "Explaining Bargaining Impasse: The Role of Self-serving Biases" (1997) 11(1) *Journal of Economic Perspectives* 109 at 119 to 121.

13. *Storrs Lectures*, see above note 11 at 1850 to 1851.

14. Daniel Watkins, "A Nudge to Mediate: How Adjustments in Choice Architecture Can Lead to Better Dispute Resolution Decisions" (2010) 4 *The American Journal of Mediation* 1 ("*Daniel Watkins*") at 16.

15. *Storrs Lectures*, see above note 11 at 1845 to 1848.

16. John Crawley, "From Grievance to Resolution Using the Nudge Principle in Mediation" (December 2010) <https://www.mediate.com//articles/cmpresolutionsBL20101206.cfm> (accessed 21 May 2019) ("*Crawley*") at 7.

17. *Storrs Lectures*, see above note 11 at 1842 to 1845; *Sunstein*, see above note 8 at 1193 to 1194.

18. *Storrs Lectures*, see above note 11 at 1842 to 1846.

19. *Daniel Watkins*, see above note 14 at 19.

20. Linda Babcock & George Loewenstein, "Explaining Bargaining Impasse: The Role of Self-serving Biases" (1997) 11(1) *Journal of Economic Perspectives* 109 at 110.

21. Chief Justice Sundaresh Menon, "Mediation and the Rule of Law: Key Note Address by the Honourable the Chief Justice Sundaresh Menon, Supreme Court of Singapore", The Law Society Mediation Forum (10 March 2017) <https://www.supremecourt.gov.sg/Data/Editor/Documents/Keynote%20Address%20-%20Mediation%20and%20the%20Rule%20of%20Law%20(Final%20edition%20after%20delivery%20-%20090317).pdf> (accessed 26 April 2018).

22. Dame Hazel Genn, "Why the Privatisation of Civil Justice is a Rule of Law Issue", 36th F A Mann Lecture, Lincoln's Inn (19 November 2012) <http://www.cnmd.ac.uk/laws/judicial-institute/layout-components/36th_F_A_Mann_Lecture_19.11.12_Professor_Hazel_Genn.pdf> (accessed 6 April 2018) at 16 to 17.
23. See generally State Courts Practice Directions, Part VI: Alternative Dispute Resolution at paragraph 35(9).
24. State Courts Practice Directions at paragraph 35(9).
25. State Courts Practice Directions at paragraphs 20(7)(b)(ii), 26(3), 36(4) and 36(9).
26. Legal Profession Professional Conduct Rules 2015 (Cap 161, No. S 706) R 17(2)(e)(ii).
27. *Thaler et al.*, see above note 5 at 434 to 435.
28. State Courts Practice Directions, Form 7.
29. Supreme Court Practice Directions, Appendix I.
30. John Crawley, "New Year's Resolution" (January 2011) <https://www.mediate.com//articles/cmpresolutionsBL20110103.cfm> (accessed 21 May 2019).
31. Ibid.
32. *Thaler et al.*, see above note 5 at 435 to 437.
33. Danielle Timmermans, "The Impact of Task Complexity on Information Use in Multi-attribute Decision Making" (June 1993) 6(2) *Journal of Behavioral Decision Making* 95 at 107 to 110.
34. *Thaler et al.*, see above note 5 at 431 to 433.
35. *Thaler et al.*, see above note 5 at 433.
36. Chief Justice Sundaresh Menon, "Building Sustainable Mediation Programmes: A Singapore Perspective", Asia-Pacific International Mediation Summit in New Delhi, India (14 February 2015) <https://www.supremecourt.gov.sg/docs/default-source/default-document-library/media-room/asia-pacific-international-mediation-summit---speech-by-cj.pdf%20target=> (accessed 16 April 2018) ("*Menon*") at paragraphs 49 to 51; *Crawley*, see above note 16.
37. *Menon*, see above note 36 at paragraphs 49 to 51.
38. *Menon*, see above note 36 at paragraphs 41 to 48.
39. Sheena S. Iyengar & Mark R. Lepper, "When Choice is Demotivating: Can One Desire Too Much of a Good Thing?" (2000) 79(6) *Journal of Personality and Social Psychology* 995 at 1003 to 1004.
40. *Nadja*, see above note 3 at 415 to 416.

130 *Contemporary Issues in Mediation Volume 4*

41. Ibid.
42. *Nadja*, see above note 3 at 413 to 415.
43. Under the Korean Commercial Arbitration Board and Beijing Arbitration Commission rules, parties may apply for mediation. Korean Commercial Arbitration Board, "Mediation Procedure" (2014) <http://www.kcab.or.kr/jsp/kcab_eng/mediation/medi_02_ex.jsp> (accessed 7 April 2018); Beijing Arbitration Commission, "About Us, Introduction" <http://www.bjac.org.cn/english/page/gybh/introduce_index.html> (accessed 7 April 2018).
44. Michael Leathes & Deborah Masucci, "The Dispute Resolution Dilemma: Opt-In or Opt-Out", Kluwer Mediation Blog (18 May 2014) < http://mediationblog.kluwerarbitration.com/2014/04/14/nudging-cross-border-mediation-forward/> (accessed 6 April 2018) ("*Leathes & Masucci*").
45. Rule 9 requires that claims exceeding $75,000 administered by AAA will be mediated concurrently with the arbitration unless parties opt-out. *Leathes & Masucci*, see above note 44.
46. Dr. Markus Altenkirch & Anindya Basarkod, "Arb-Med-Arb: What is It and How Can It Help the Parties to Solve Their Disputes Efficiently?", *Lexology* (20 November 2017) <https://www.lexology.com/library/detail.aspx?g=ffa5d715-f4b4-4cc0-af45-b3a7dc6a0789> (accessed 6 April 2018).

Chapter 2 Mediation, Legal Education and the Adversarial Culture in Singapore

1. Justice Belinda Ang, Opening Remarks at SMU Research Forum, "Expanding the Scope of Dispute Resolution and Access to Justice: The Use of Mediation Within the Courts" (12 March 2018) at [5] <http://www.mediation.com.sg/assets/downloads/expanding-the-scope-of-dispute-resolution-and-access-to-justice-the-use-of-mediation-within-the-courts/Justice-Ang-UseofMediation-Within-the-Courts-For-Publication-19.3.18.pdf> (accessed 28 March 2018) ("*Ang*").
2. For instance, the Singapore International Mediation Centre, Singapore Mediation Centre and the State Courts Centre for Dispute Resolution; see generally *Ang*, above at note 1; Chief Justice Sundaresh Menon, Speech at the Opening of the Singapore International Mediation Centre (5 November 2014) at [15]-[16] <http://simc.com.sg/wp-content/uploads/2014/11/Opening-of-the-Singapore-International-Mediation-Centre-on-5-November-20....pdf> (accessed 28 March 2018); Chief Justice Sundaresh Menon, Speech at the Joint Launch of the State Courts Centre for Dispute

Resolution and "Mediation in Singapore: A Practical Guide" (4 March 2015) <https://www.statecourts.gov.sg/Lawyer/Documents/State%20Courts%20 -%20Launch%20of%20State%20Courts%20Centre%20for%20Dispute%20 Resolution%20Speech%20on%204%20March%202015.pdf> (accessed 28 March 2018).

3. The comments in this chapter do not extend to legal education at other law schools in Singapore as the author's knowledge is restricted to the curriculum at the Faculty of Law, National University of Singapore.

4. L.A. Sheridan, "Legal Education" (1961) 27 *Malayan Law Journal* at 6–7; see also Philip Nalliah Pillai, *Legal Education in Singapore: It's Development, Problem and Prospects* (Singapore: Maruzen International, 1980) at 9–10, who cites Sheridan, "University Law" (1956) *Malaya Law Review* xxviii.

5. Indranee Rajah S.C., Senior Minister of State for Law and Finance, Speech at the Launch of the NUS Law Centre for Pro Bono and Clinical Legal Education (31 October 2017) at [2] <http://www.nas.gov.sg/archivesonline/ data/pdfdoc/20171031012/Speech%20by%20SMS%20-%20NUS%20 Pro%20Bono%20and%20Clinical%20Legal%20Education%2031%20 Oct%202017.pdf> (accessed 15 March 2018); At the same event, NUS law school dean Professor Simon Chesterman also remarked, "Clinical legal education takes student learning beyond the classroom to work with real people, real problems, and real consequences. Students work with practising lawyers to draft affidavits and documents that they see being used in court. These clinical faculty bring professional expertise into the law school, helping students to develop the art and craft of lawyering". See "NUS Law Launches New Centre for Pro Bono & Clinical Legal Education", NUS News (31 October 2017) <https://news.nus.edu.sg/press-releases/pro-bono-clinical-legal-education> (accessed 15 March 2018) ("*NUS News*"); see also Amelia Teng, "NUS Revamps Law Course to Broaden Knowledge, Skills", *The Straits Times* (31 January 2014) <http://www.asiaone.com/news/edvantage/nus-revamps-law-course-broaden-knowledge-skills> (accessed 15 March 2018) ("*Teng*") ; Joint Press Release by Legal Aid Bureau and NUS (6 October 2010) <https://www.mlaw.gov.sg/content/dam/minlaw/corp/ assets/documents/NUS-LAB-PR.pdf> (accessed 15 March 2018);

6. Professor Chesterman said "You'll see that the rewards of being a lawyer go far beyond the money you make" (*Teng*, see above note 5); and "We hope to create more opportunities for our students to see the law in action — and learn that the value of a lawyer is measured in people helped rather than hours billed" (*NUS News*, see above note 5).

132 *Contemporary Issues in Mediation Volume 4*

7. *Teng*, see above note 5.

8. Indranee Rajah S.C., Senior Minister of State for Law and Finance, Opening Address at the Singapore International Arbitration Centre Hard Talk 2017 (12 October 2017) at [16(c)] <https://www.mlaw.gov.sg/content/minlaw/en/news/speeches/opening-address-sms-indranee-siac-hard-talk-2017.html> (accessed 19 March 2018).

9. Brad Berenson, Vice President, Litigation & Legal Policy at General Electric Company, "The Mediation Imperative: Why Successful Companies Cannot Afford to Ignore Mediation", Singapore Mediation Lecture 2014 (8 October 2014) at 13 <http://www.mediation.com.sg/assets/downloads/singapore-mediation-lecture-2014/02-Berenson-Singapore-Lecture-Sept-25-2014.pdf> (accessed 28 March 2018) ("*Berenson*").

10. "Legal Foundations of Mediation" in Danny McFadden & George Lim, eds., Mediation in Singapore: A Practical Guide (Singapore: Sweet & Maxwell, 2017) ("Mediation in Singapore") para [8.010] at 208.

11. *Berenson*, see above note 9 at 7.

12. Id at 17.

13. See Letter from the Dean, (NUS Law) at 3 <https://issuu.com/nuslaw/docs/letter_from_the_dean_2018> (accessed 29 March 2018).

14. Chief Justice Sundaresh Menon, Speech at the NUS Faculty of Law 60th Anniversary Gala (20 October 2017) at [10] <https://www.supremecourt.gov.sg/Data/Editor/Documents/The%20NUS%20Faculty%20of%20Law%2060th%20Anniversary%20Speech%20(Final%20-%202010171).pdf> (accessed 27 March 2018) ("*Menon — NUS 60th Anniversary*"); see also Richard Susskind, *Tomorrow's Lawyers: An Introduction to your Future* (Oxford: Oxford University Press, 2017) ("*Susskind*").

15. *Ang*, see above note 1 at [2].

16. *Parliamentary Debates Singapore: Official Report* Vol 94 at 32 (10 January 2017) (Senior Minister of State for Law: Indranee Rajah S.C.)

17. Ibid.

18. Indranee Rajah SC, Senior Minister of State for Law and Finance, Opening Address at the Community Mediation Centre's Mediator's Appointment Ceremony and Appreciation Dinner (1 December 2015) at [19] <https://www.mlaw.gov.sg/content/cmc/en/media-room/speeches/opening-address-by-senior-minister-of-state-for-law-and-finance-.html> (accessed 27 March 2018).

19. Former Chief Justice Chan Sek Keong, Speech at the Launch of the SMU Centre for Dispute Resolution (16 April 2009) at [6] <https://www.supremecourt.gov.sg/

news/speeches/launch-of-the-smu---centre-for-dispute-resolution----speech-by-chief-justice-chan-sek-keong> (accessed 27 March 2018).

20. Id at [7]; see also generally Ho Peng Kee, Mediation Symposium Keynote Address (20 May 2016) <http://www.mediation.com.sg/news-and-views/news-and-speeches/mediation-symposium-keynote-address/> (accessed 17 March 2018) (*"Ho Peng Kee"*).

21. Dorcas Quek & Kenneth Choo, "Mediation Advocacy for Civil Disputes in the Subordinate Courts: Perspectives from the Bench", *Singapore Law Gazette* (September 2012) at 14 (*"Quek & Choo"*); *Menon — NUS 60th Anniversary*, see above note 14 at [15].

22. Andrew Phang JA suggests that this might be a problem of the common law generally; see Justice of Appeal Andrew Phang, Speech at the 4th Asian Mediation Association Conference, "Mediation and the Courts — The Singapore Experience"(20 October 2016) at [1] <https://www.supremecourt.gov.sg/Data/Editor/Documents/Keynote%20Speech%20-%204th%20Asian%20Mediation%20Conference.pdf> (accessed 19 March 2018).

23. *Quek & Choo*, see above note 21 at 14.

24. *Ho Peng Kee*, see above note 20.

25. National Alternative Dispute Resolution Advisory Council, Teaching Alternative Dispute Resolution in Australian Law Schools (Canberra, Australian Government Attorney General's Department, 2012) ("NADRAC") at 5.

26. Kathy Douglas, "The Role of ADR in Developing Lawyer's Practice: Lessons from Australian Legal Education" (2015) 22 *International Journal of the Legal Profession* 71 at 75–76 (*"Douglas"*).

27. See generally Tania Sourdin, "Not Teaching ADR in Law Schools? Implications for Law Students, Clients and the ADR Field" (1 April 2012) Available at SSRN: https://ssrn.com/abstract=2721539.

28. In the four year undergraduate LLB program at NUS, students spend the first two years reading compulsory courses. In their upper years, students are free to read any elective they wish (although they also have to complete the course on the Law of Evidence).

29. This refers to Criminal Law, Law of Contract, Law of Torts, Company Law, Constitutional and Administrative Law, Equity and Trusts and Principles of Property Law courses <https://law.nus.edu.sg/student_matters/course_listing/compulsory_subject.html> (accessed 18 March 2018).

30. This refers to Legal Analysis, Research & Communication, Trial Advocacy or Corporate Deals.

31. Namely, Singapore Law in Context, Introduction to Legal Theory, Legal Systems of Asia; the word "fluff" often has the negative connotation of describing something as being lacking in substance. It is also commonly used as a term to describe a non-substantive law course. Here it is put in quotation marks because these courses do not actually lack content, but their being labelled as "fluff" may be arguably attributed to the inability of the young law student to fully appreciate the nuances and intricacies of these areas of study.

32. See for example, Gary L. Blasi, "What Lawyers Know: Lawyering Expertise, Cognitive Science, and the Functions of Theory" (1995) 4 *Journal of Legal Education* 313.

33. Jess Krannich, James Holbrook & Jule McAdams, "Beyond Thinking Like a Lawyer and the Traditional Legal Paradigm: Toward a Comprehensive View of Legal Education" (2009) 86 *Denver University Law Review* 381 at 382 ("*Krannich et al.*"); see also Julie Marcfarlane, *The New Lawyer: How Settlement is Transforming the Practice of Law* (Vancouver, BC: UBC Press, 2008) at 226: "For the most part, law schools do not see themselves as teaching students about how to be a lawyer, what that might be like, what choices and challenges they might face in practice, but rather, how to "think like a lawyer." This bifurcation between "thinking" and "doing" is reflected in an apparently interminable and seemingly inconclusive debate over the extent to which the law curriculum should be driven by the exigencies of legal practice.

34. *Krannich et al.*, see above note 33 at 389.

35. Linda Heng, "Psychology and the Interest-Based Model of Mediation" in *Mediation in Singapore*, see above note 10 at para [6.006-7]; see also Indranee Rajah S.C., Senior Minister of State for Law, Speech at the Launch of the Singapore International Mediation Institute (5 November 2014) at [11] <https://www.mlaw.gov.sg/content/minlaw/en/news/speeches/SMS-speech-at-SIMI-launch.html> (accessed 20 March 2018).

36. Available at https://libportal.nus.edu.sg/frontend/index (login required).

37. "Legal Foundations of Mediation" in *Mediation in Singapore*, see above note 10 at para [8.010-13].

38. A client might lose if he chooses to enforce his contractual rights at the expense of an ongoing business relationship that he needs for his company to continue as a going-concern.

39. For example, to file a claim in Tort rather than Contract, such as in cases involving misrepresentation.

40. Joel Lee, "Responding to Conflict", *Kluwer Mediation Blog* (14 January 2015) <http://mediationblog.kluwerarbitration.com/2015/01/14/responding-to-conflict/> (accessed 23 March 2018).

End Notes   135

41. The Singapore Law in Context course contains a brief introduction to ADR, but does not go into much detail.

42. See "Course Listing" <https://law.nus.edu.sg/student_matters/course_listing/courses_desc.asp?MC=LC2013&Sem=2&MGC=1> (accessed 3 April 2018).

43. As of Academic Year 2017/2018, the course in Mediation has a cap of 24 students per class.

44. Chief Justice Sundaresh Menon, Speech at the Global Pound Conference Series 2016, "Shaping the Future of Dispute Resolution & Improving Access to Justice"(17 March 2016) at [23] <https://www.supremecourt.gov.sg/Data/Editor/Documents/%5BFinal%5D%20Global%20Pound%20Conference%20Series%202016%20-%20'Shaping%20the%20Future%20of%20Dispute%20Resolution%20%20Improving%20Access%20to%20Justice'.pdf> (accessed 18 March 2018).

45. John Lande & Jean Sternlight, "The Potential Contribution of ADR to an Integrated Curriculum: Preparing Law Students for Real World Lawyering" (2010) 25 *Ohio State Journal on Dispute Resolution* 247 at 256.

46. *Ho Peng Kee*, see above note 20.

47. *Menon — NUS 60th Anniversary*, see above note 14 at [6].

48. *Menon — NUS 60th Anniversary*, see above note 14 at [10], citing *Susskind*, see above note 14.

49. Lillian Corbin, Paula Baron & Judy Gutman, "ADR Zealots, Adjudicative Romantics and Everything in Between: Lawyers in Mediations" (2015) 38(2) *University of New South Wales Law Journal* 492 at 512.

50. NADRAC, see above note 25.

51. Webb, J., Ching, J. Maharg, P. & Sherr, A., "Setting Standards; The Future of Legal Services Education and Training Regulation in England and Wales" (Legal Education and Training Review, 2013).

52. William Sullivan, Anne Colby, Judith Wegner, Lloyd Bond & Lee Shulman, eds., *Educating Lawyers: Preparation for the Profession of Law* (John Wiley and Sons, 2007); *Douglas*, see above note 26 at 74.

53. Mary Keyes & Richard Johnstone, "Changing Legal Education: Rhetoric, Reality, and Prospects for the Future" (2004) 26(4) *Sydney Law Review* 537 at 550.

54. *Menon — NUS 60th Anniversary*, see above note 14 at [6], [10].

55. Indranee Rajah, Senior Minister of State for Law and Finance, Closing Address at the Global Pound Conference Singapore 2016 (18 March 2016) at [19] <https://www.mlaw.gov.sg/content/minlaw/en/news/speeches/closing-address-by-ms-indranee-rajah--senior-minister-of-state-f.html> (accessed 18 March 2018).

Chapter 3 A Comparative Guide to Drafting Enforceable Mediation Clauses

1. The use of the term re-emergence is deliberate. Resort to ADR to resolve conflicts can be traced back to ancient Phoenicians who use these mechanisms to resolve trade disputes. Moreover, in Southeast Asian cultures, such as Singapore, resort to mediation to resolve conflicts is a cultural norm. See Jerome Barret & Joseph Barrett, *A History of Alternative Dispute Resolution: The Story of a Political, Social and Cultural Movement* (San Francisco: Jossey-Bass, 2004) at 71; Richard Birke & Louise E. Teitz, "US Mediation in the Twenty-First Century: The Path That Brought America to Uniform Laws and Mediation in Cyberspace" in Nadja Alexander, ed., *Global Trends in Mediation* (Germany: Centrale Für Mediation, 2003) at 365.

2. Such as the International Chamber of Commerce (ICC), Association for International Arbitration (AIA), Center for Effective Dispute Resolution (CEDR), International Institute for Conflict Prevention & Resolution (CPR), Dutch Mediation Institute (NMI), International Mediation Institute (IMI), etc.

3. Multi-tiered dispute resolution, also known as "(multi-) step", "ADR first" or "escalation" clauses, are used to refer to a dispute resolution agreement that contains multiple tiers of dispute resolution mechanisms, usually commencing with non-binding processes such as negotiation or mediation before calling for arbitration or litigation.

4. See Oliver Krauss, "The Enforceability of Escalation Clauses Providing for Negotiations in Good Faith under English Law" (2016) 2(1) *McGill Journal of Dispute Resolution* 142 at 144; David Cairns, "Mediating International Commercial Disputes: Differences in U.S. And European Approaches" (2005) 60(3) *Dispute Resolution Journal* 62 at 64.

5. See Didem Kayali, "Enforceability of Multi-Tiered Dispute Resolution Clauses" (2010) 27(6) *Journal of International Arbitration* 551 at 552; Horst Eidenmüeller & Helge Groserichter, "Alternative Dispute Resolution and Private International Law" (31 July 2015) at 8. Available at SSRN: https://ssrn.com/abstract=2638471.

6. Christian Bühring-Uhle, Lars Kirchhoff & Gabriele Scherer, *Arbitration and Mediation in International Business* (The Netherlands: Alphen aan den Rijn, 2006) at 229; Alexander Jollies, "Consequences of Multi-Tier Arbitration Clauses: Issues of Enforcement" (2006) 72(4) *Arbitration* at 329.

7. White v Kampner, 641 Atlantic Reporter Second Series 1381 (Conn 1994), 1387: Court invalidating arbitral award in light of a mandatory negotiation requirement.

End Notes   137

8. From 1999–2005, there was a 120% increase in the number of litigations regarding mediation issues (see James R. Coben & Peter N. Thompson, "Mediation Litigation Trends: 1999–2007" (2007) 1(3) *World Arbitration & Mediation Review* 395 at 398).

9. Nadja Alexander, *International and Comparative Mediation: Legal Perspectives* (New York: Kluwer Law International, 2009) ("*Nadja*") at 174.

10. Maud Piers, "Europe's Role in Alternative Dispute Resolution: Off to a Good Start?" (2014) 2 *Journal of Dispute Resolution* 269 ("*Piers*") at 295; Laurence Boulle, *Mediation: Principles, Process, Practice* (Australia: Ligare Pty Ltd., 3rd Edition, 2011) ("*Boulle*") at 617; Anne Bihancov, "What Is An Example of a Good Dispute Resolution Clause and Why?" (2014) *Australian Centre for Justice Innovation* ("*Bihancov*") at 2.

11. *Piers*, see above note 10 at 295; *Boulle*, see above note 10 at 617.

12. These include Austria, Australia, England & Wales, Germany, Singapore, the Netherlands and the United States.

13. Ronán Feehily, "The Contractual Certainty of Commercial Agreements to Mediate in Ireland" (2016) 6(1) *Irish Journal of Legal Studies* 59 at 64. Also see for Germany, BGH, XII ZR 165/06, at [27–28] (mediation clauses prevent court action) and the United States case severing the agreement to mediate from the rest of MDR clause to save the MDR: Templeton Development Corp. v. Superior Court, 144 California Appellate Reports 4th 1073, 1084, 51 California Reporter 3d 19, 27 (2006).

14. Also see New South Wales Court of Appeals, United Group Rail Service Ltd v Rail Corporation New South Wales [2009] New South Wales Court of Appeal 177 at [89].

15. Zheng Sophia Tang, *Jurisdiction and Arbitration Agreements in International Commercial Law* (New York: Routledge, 2014) at 74.

16. This includes considerations such as whether the agreement has to be in writing, signed, in a special font or colour, stapled or digital. Substantive (or material) validity concerns the legality of the content of the parties' agreement, their capacity and consent to enter the agreement, public policy and sufficient certainty.

17. On 10 January 2017, Singapore passed the Mediation Act (MA). The MA is a legislative framework for commercial mediation that is connected to Singapore. According to Section 4(3) of the MA 2017, for a mediation clause to fall within the scope of the statute, it must be in writing.

18. Frank Diedrich, "International/Cross-Border Mediation within the EU — Place of Mediation, Qualifications of the Mediator and the Applicable Law"

in Frank Diedrich, ed., *The Status Quo of Mediation in Europe and Overseas: Options for Countries in Transition* (Hamburg: Verlga Dr. Kovač, 2014) at 63.

19. In the context of EU Member States, also see Regulation (EC) No. 593/2008 of the European Parliament and of the Council of 17 June 2008 on the law applicable to contractual obligations (Rome I), Articles 3 & 4.

20. Charles Jarrosson, "Legal Issues Raised by ADR" in C. Goldsmith, Arnold Ingen-Housz & Gerald H. Pointon, eds., *ADR in Business: Practice and Issues across Countries and Cultures* (The Netherlands: Kluwer Law International, 2011) ("*Jarrosson*") at 115.

21. *Nadja*, see above note 9 at 187. Also see Articles 19(4) and 20 of the Basic Law of the Federal Republic of Germany (Grundgesetz für die Bundesrepublik Deutschland), 23 May 1949 regarding unverzichtbare Rechte.

22. See BGH, VIII ZR 344/97, Judgement of 18 November 1998; OLG Rostock, 3 U 37/06, Judgement of 19 September 2006 at II.

23. European Court of Justice, Alassini v. Telecom Italia SpA, Judgement of 18 March 2010, Joined cases C-317/08 and 320/08.

24. Joined cases C-317/08 and 320/08 at [68].

25. *Jarrosson*, see above note 20 at 115.

26. General principles of contract formation under the common law require the parties to a contract to demonstrate a clear intent to enter into a relation that is sufficiently certain in its terms (Bihancov, see above note 10 at 2; Keith Han & Nicholas Poon, "The Enforceability of Alternative Dispute Resolution Agreements: Emerging Problems and Issues" (2013) *Singapore Academy of Law Journal* 25 ("*Han & Poon*") at 457).

27. Wian Erlank, "Enforcement of Multi-Tiered Dispute Resolution Clauses" (9 September 2002) at 42. Available at SSRN: https://ssrn.com/abstract=1491027 ("*Erlank*").

28. International Chamber of Commerce (ICC) Case No. 4230: The tribunal found that it had jurisdiction in accordance with the non-obligatory wording of the clause: "all disputes related to the present contract may be settled amicably." ICC Case No. 10256: The tribunal found that the wording of the clause indicated that mediation was not mandatory: "either party […] may refer the dispute to an expert for consideration of the dispute."

29. *Erlank*, see above note 27 at 42.

30. In Austria, the predominant form of dispute resolution is litigation in front of national courts (Peter G. Mayr & Nemeth Kristin, "Regulation of Dispute Resolution in Austria: A Traditional Litigation Culture Slowly Embraces ADR" in Felix Steffek & Hannes Unberath, eds., *Regulating Dispute Resolution: ADR and Access to Justice at the Crossroads* (Oxford: Hart

Publishing Ltd., 2013) at 65). Likewise, litigation is the most common form of dispute resolution in Germany. Recourse to court is a deeply rooted tradition in German legal culture, as Germany has a traditionally strong court system (Burkhard Hess & Nils Pelzer, "Regulation of Dispute Resolution in Germany: Cautious Steps Towards the Construction of an ADR System" in Felix Steffek & Hannes Unberath, eds., *Regulating Dispute Resolution: ADR and Access to Justice at the Crossroads* (Oxford: Hart Publishing Ltd., 2013) at 212; Arthur Trossen, "Practical Issues and Shortcomings of the New 2012 German Mediation Act" in Frank Diedrich, ed., *The Status Quo of Mediation in Europe and Overseas: Options for Countries in Transition* (Hamburg: Verlga Dr. Kovač, 2014) at 118; Iris Benöhr, Christopher Hodges & Naomi Creutzfeldt-Banda, "Germany" in Christopher Hodges, Iris Benöhr & Naomi Creutzfeldt-Banda, eds., *Consumer ADR in Europe Civil Justice Systems* (Oxford: Hart Publishing Ltd., 2012) at 73).

31. The mutual agreement not to sue (*dilatorischer Klageverzicht*) is a procedural law agreement that is understood as a temporary waiver of the parties' inherent right to go to court. Such an agreement does not affect the merits of the dispute (Peter Klaus Berger, *Private Dispute Resolution in International Business: Negotiation, Mediation, Arbitration*, Vol. 1 (The Netherlands: Alphen aan Den Rijn, 2015) at 128).

32. BGB §145 et seq. It should be noted that the conditions of defining the dispute subject to ADR is known as the *Bestimmtheitserfordernis* and is highly relevant in ADR agreements where parties agree to resolve a future dispute via ADR. Also see *Piers*, above note 10 at 287.

33. *Piers*, see above note 10 at 288.

34. The BGH has held conciliation clauses that clearly demonstrate the intention of the parties to make litigation a last resort as enforceable.

35. Hugh Beale, "Characteristics of Contract Laws and the European Optional Instrument" in Horst Eidenmüeller, ed., *Regulator Competition in Contract Law and Dispute Resolution* (Oxford: Oxford University Publishers, 2013) at 320.

36. Joel Lee, "Mediation Clauses at the Crossroads" (2001) *Singapore Journal of Legal Studies* 81 at 87; *Han & Poon*, see above note 26 at 474.

37. Neil Andrews, *Andrews on Civil Processes: Arbitration and Mediation*, Vol. 2, (Cambridge: Cambridge University Press, 2013) at para. [1.5.2].

38. Sulamerica CIA Nacionla De Seguros SA v Enesa Engenharia SA [2012] Court of Appeal of England and Wales (Civil Division) 638 ("*Sulamerica v Enesa*").

39. *Sulamerica v Enesa*, see above note 38 at [35–36].

140   *Contemporary Issues in Mediation Volume 4*

40. Wah (Aka Alan Tang) & Anor v Grant Thornton International Ltd. and others, [2012] High Court of England and Wales (Chancery Division) 3198 ("*Wah v Grant Thornton*").

41. *Wah v Grant Thornton*, see above note 40 at [27] for the dispute resolution clause and [63 & 82].

42. Cable & Wireless Plc v IBM United Kingdom Ltd [2002] High Court of England and Wales (Commercial Court) 2059 ("*Cable v IBM*").

43. *Cable v IBM*, see above note 42 at [25].

44. Emirates Trading Agency LLC v Prime Mineral Exports Private Ltd [2014] High Court of England and Wales (Commercial Court) 014 (Queen's Bench Division).

45. See also Maryam Salehijam, "Enforceability Of ADR Agreements: An Analysis Of Selected EU Member States" (2018) *International Trade and Business Law Review*.

46. International Research Corp PLC v Lufthansa Systems Asia Pacific Pte Ltd [2013] Singapore Court of Appeal 55 ("*IRC v Lufthansa — CA*").

47. *IRC v Lufthansa — CA*, see above note 46 at [54].

48. International Research Corp PLC v Lufthansa Systems Asia Pacific Pte Ltd and another [2012] Singapore High Court 226, at [95].

49. Andrew Murray, Presentation at NSW Chapter Event, "Enforcing the Modern Suite of Dispute Resolution Clauses" (2015) at 3.

50. In interpreting clauses in commercial contracts, the courts apply the following rules of interpretation: "Give the contract a business-like interpretation paying attention to the language used by the parties, the commercial circumstance which the document addresses, and the object which it is intended to secure" (Mccann v Switzeland Insurance Australia Limited [2000] Commonwealth Law Reports 65); "Only hold a clause void for uncertainty as a last resort, where it is not possible to give it a reasonable meaning" (Lord Denning MR in Greater London Council v Connolly [1970] 2 Queen's Bench Division 100).

51. WTE Co-Generation v RCR Energy Pty Ltd [2013] Victorian Supreme COurt 314, at [46].

52. In Aiton, Einstein J noted that "if specificity beyond essential certainty were required, the dispute resolution procedure may be counter-productive as it may begin to look much like litigation itself." However, the clause in this case fail, as it did not address the repayment of the mediator (Aiton Australia Pty Ltd v Transfield Pty Ltd, [1999] Supreme Court of New South Wales 996 ("*Aiton v Transfield*") at [46 &174]). Also see Mike Hales, "Australia" in International Bar Association Litigation Committee, *Multi-Tiered Dispute Resolution Clauses* (2015) at 11.

End Notes   141

53. "A state of mind consisting in (1) honesty in belief or purpose, (2) faithfulness to one's duty or obligation, (3) observance of reasonable commercial standards of fair dealing in a given trade or business or (4) absence of intent to defraud or to seek unconscionable advantage" (Bryan A. Garner, ed., *Black's Law Dictionary*, 7th ed., (US: St. Paul, 1999) at 701).
54. Chris Parker, Gregg Rowan & Nich Pantlin, "How Far Can You Act in Your Own Self-Interest?" (2015) Herbert Smith Freehills at 3.
55. See *Sulamerica v Enesa*, above note 38. Also see *Han & Poon*, above note 26 at 469; Thomas Heintzman, "When Is a Mediation Agreement Enforceable?" (2012) <http://www.heintzmanadr.com/international-commercial-arbitration/when-is-a-mediation-agreement-enforceable/> (accessed 13 October 2017).
56. *Aiton v Transfield*, see above note 52 at [67].
57. *Erlank*, see above note 27 at 29.
58. The use of the words "shall" and "must" in a dispute resolution clause indicates that the parties must first seek mediation before arbitration (compulsory).
59. See also ICC Case No. 9984: The wording of the clause indicated that the ADR is an obligation, the tribunals found the clause binding upon the parties.

Chapter 4 Enforcing Mediation Settlement Agreements: An Examination of the Draft Convention on International Settlement Agreements Resulting from Mediation

1. Florence D'Souza, *Knowledge, Mediation and Empire* (Oxford University Press, 2015) at 147.
2. Ian Macduff, *Essays on Mediation* (Wolters Kluwer, 2016) at p 29.
3. United Nations Commission on International Trade Law, Sixty-seventh Session (2017) UN Doc A/CN.9/WG.II/WP.202/Add.1 (*"Sixty-seventh Session with Addendum"*) at 2.
4. Id at 3.
5. United Nations Commission on International Trade Law, Sixty-seventh Session (2017) UN Doc A/CN.9/WG.II/WP.202/ (*"Sixty-seventh Session"*) at 3.
6. United Nations Commission on International Trade Law, Fifty-first Session (2017) UN Doc A/CN.9/929/ (*"Fifty-first Session"*) at 5.
7. Id at 4.
8. *Sixty-seventh Session*, see above note 5 at 4.
9. Ibid.

10. Convention of 30 June 2005 on Choice of Court Agreements 44 *International Legal Materials* 1294 (2005) at Article 9.
11. New York Arbitration Convention website <http://www.newyorkconvention.org/countries> (accessed 17 November 2017).
12. (1829) 9 B.&C. 840, at 850.
13. Grigori Lazarev, "Settlement Farm", Thomson Reuters (August 2016) <http://arbitrationblog.practicallaw.com/settlement-farm-should-some-settlement-agreements-be-more-equal-than-others-the-uncitrals-proposed-new-instrument-on-the-enforcement-of-international-commercial-settlemen/> (accessed 17 November 2017).
14. *Fifty-first Session*, see above note 6 at 4.
15. *Sixty-seventh Session*, see above note 5 at 5.
16. Law Reform Committee, "Report of the Law Reform Committee on the Hague Convention on Choice of Court Agreements 2005", Singapore Academy of Law (March 2013) <https://www.sal.org.sg/Portals/0/PDF%20Files/Law%20Reform/Report%20of%20the%20Law%20Reform%20Committee%20on%20the%20Hague%20Convention%20on%20Choice%20of%20Court%20Agreements%202005.pdf> (accessed 17 November 2017) at [16].
17. *Sixty-seventh Session with Addendum*, see above note 3 at 5.
18. Dorcas Quek Anderson, Nadja Alexander (Editor), and Anna Howard (Associate Editor), "UNCITRAL and the enforceability of iMSAs: the debate heats up — Part 2", *Kluwer Mediation Blog*, (September 2016) <http://mediationblog.kluwerarbitration.com/2016/09/21/uncitral-and-the-enforceability-of-imsas-the-debate-heats-up-part-2/> (accessed 17 November 2017) ("*UNCITRAL Part 2*").
19. Nadja Alexander, *International and Comparative Mediation: Legal Perspectives* (Kluwer Law International, 2009) at 48 ("*International and Comparative Mediation*").
20. Ibid.
21. Vivienne Harpwood, *Modern Tort Law* (Routledge, 2009) at 382.
22. Nadja Alexander, *Mediation Essentials* (International Finance Corporation, 2016) at 41 ("*Mediation Essentials*").
23. Arthur W. Rovine, *Contemporary Issues in International Arbitration and Mediation: The Fordham Papers 2013* (Brill, 2015) at 472.
24. Robyn Caroll, "Apologies as a Legal Remedy" (2013) 35 *Sydney Law Review* 317 at 318.
25. Chitty, *Chitty on Contracts* (Sweet & Maxwell, 2012) at 1911; *Cud v Rutter* [1719] 1 Peere Williams' Reports 570.

26. German Civil Code (2002).

27. French Civil Code (2004).

28. Herbert Kronke, *Recognition and Enforcement of Foreign Arbitral Awards* (Kluwer Law International, 2010) at 310.

29. *Mediation Essentials*, see above note 22 at 62; David Spencer, *Mediation Law and Practice* (Cambridge University Press, 2007) at 475.

30. Gary Born, *International Commercial Arbitration* (Kluwer Law International, 2001) at 860; In the Matter of an Arbitration Under the Arbitration Agreement (Croatia v Slovenia) [2016] Permanent Court of Arbitration Case No 2012-04 (Partial Award) at [177]–[183].

31. *UNCITRAL Part 2*, see above note 18.

32. UNCITRAL, *UNCITRAL Model Law on International Commercial Conciliation with Guide to Enactment and Use 2002* (United Nations Publication, 2004) at 12.

33. Singapore Parliamentary Debates, Official Report (10 January 2017) vol 94 at [17].

34. International Mediation Institute website <http://www.imimediation.org/tag/survey/> ("IMI website") (accessed 17 November 2017).

35. Singapore International Arbitration centre website <http://www.siac.org.sg/model-clauses/the-singapore-arb-med-arb-clause/> (accessed 17 November 2015).

36. Singapore Mediation Act 2017 (No. 1 of 2017), section 11(2).

37. *International and Comparative Mediation*, see above note 19 at 77.

Chapter 5 Mediator Neutrality in Singapore: The Siren Call for a Paradigm Shift

1. See for example Singapore International Mediation Institute Code of Professional Conduct.

2. Nadja Alexander, "The Mediation Metamodel: Understanding Practice" (2008) 26 *Conflict Resolution Quaterly* 97 at 102.

3. Linda Mulcahy, "The Possibilities and Desirability of Mediator Neutrality — Towards an Ethic of Partiality?" (2001) 10(4) *Social and Legal Studies* 505 at 511.

4. Id at 510.

5. Rachael Field, "Exploring the Potential of Contextual Ethics in Mediation" in Francesca Bartlett, Reid Mortensen & Kieran Tranter, eds., *Alternative Perspectives on Lawyers and Legal Ethics: Reimagining the Profession* (New York: Routledge, 2011) ("*Field*") at 199.

6. Laurence Boulle, *Mediation: Principles, Process, Practice* (Butterworths, 1st Edition, 1996) at 19.
7. Ibid.
8. *Field*, see above note 5 at 193.
9. Lon Fuller, "Mediation — Its Forms and Functions" (1971) 44 *South California Law Review* 305 at 305.
10. Sean Cobb & Janet Rifkin, "Practice and Paradox: Deconstructing Neutrality in Mediation" (1991) 16 *Law and Social Inquiry* 25 at 43.
11. Susan Douglas, "Neutrality in Mediation: A Study of Mediator Perceptions" (2008) 8(1) *QUT Law Review* 139 ("*Douglas*") at 147.
12. David Greatbatch & Robert Dingwall, "Selective Facilitation: Some Preliminary Observations on a Strategy Used by Divorce Mediators" (1989) 23(4) *Law and Society Review* 613 at 636.
13. *Douglas*, see above note 11 at 141.
14. Claire Baylis & Robyn Carroll, "Power Issues in Mediation" (2005) 7(8) *ADR Bulletin* 1 at 2.
15. Ibid.
16. *Field*, see above note 5 at 197.
17. Alison Taylor, "Concepts of Neutrality in Family Mediation: Contexts, Ethics, Influence and Transformative Process" (1997) 14(3) *Mediation Quarterly* 215 at 230.
18. *Field*, see above note 5 at 194.
19. *Field*, see above note 5 at 195.
20. Hilary Astor, "Mediator Neutrality: Making Sense of Theory and Practice" (2007) *Social and Legal Studies* 221 ("*Astor*") at 226.
21. *Douglas*, see above note 11 at 152.
22. Ibid.
23. *Douglas*, see above note 11 at 146.
24. *Astor*, see above note 20 at 222.
25. Rachael Field, "Mediation Ethics in Australia — A Case for Rethinking the Foundational Paradigm" (2012) 19 *James Cook University Law Review* 41 at 67.
26. *Field*, see above note 5 at 198.
27. *Field*, see above note 5 at 201.
28. Kenneth Cloke, *Mediating Dangerously: The Frontiers of Conflict Resolution* (San Francisco: Jossey-Bass, 2001) at 13.
29. *Field*, see above note 5 at 201.
30. Ibid.

31. *Field*, see above note 5 at 203.
32. *Field*, see above note 5 at 205.
33. Noel Preston, *Understanding Ethics* (Leichhardt, N.S.W.: The Federation Press, 2001) at 74.
34. *Field*, see above note 5 at 198.
35. National Mediator Accreditation Standards (NMAS) Practice Standards, Clause 2.2.
36. Rachael Field, "Rethinking Mediation Ethics: A Contextual Method to Support Party Self-Determination" (2011) 22(1) *Australasian Dispute Resolution Journal* 8 at 12.
37. Mary Ann Noone & Lola Akin Ojelabi, "Ethical Challenges for Mediators around the Globe: An Australian Perspective" (2014) 45(1) *Washington Journal of Law & Policy* 145 at 187.
38. NMAS Practice Standards, Clause 5.
39. Jonathan Crowe, "Two Models of Mediation Ethics" (2017) 39 *Sydney Law Review* 147 ("*Crowe*") at 154.
40. NMAS Practice Standards, Clause 8.8 and US Model Standards of Conduct for Mediators ("US Model Standards") Standard IX.
41. *Crowe*, see above note 39 at 155.
42. Singapore International Mediation Institute Code of Professional Conduct ("SIMI Code") Clauses 5.8 and 5.9.
43. State Courts of Singapore: Code of Ethics and Basic Principles on Court Mediation ("State Courts Code") Clause 2.3(b).
44. NMAS Practice Standards Clause 2.2.
45. US Model Standards Standard I.
46. NMAS Practice Standards Clause 6.1.
47. NMAS Practice Standards Clause 7.4.
48. NMAS Practice Standards Clause 3.2(f).
49. NMAS Practice Standards Clause 8.8.
50. US Model Standards Standard IX (B).
51. *Douglas*, see above note 11 at 139.

Chapter 6 The Case for Confidentiality: Singapore's Mediation Act

1. Bruce Pardy & Charles Pou, "Confidentiality" in Ellen Waldman, ed., *Mediation Ethics: Cases and Commentaries* (San Francisco: Jossey-Bass, 2011) ("*Pardy & Pou*") at 55.

146 *Contemporary Issues in Mediation Volume 4*

2. Ibid.

3. Bill No 37/2016.

4. See J Folberg & A Taylor, Mediation: *A Comprehensive Guide to Resolving Conflicts Without Litigation* (San Francisco: Jossey-Bass, 1984) at 264; LR Freedman & ML Prigoff, "Confidentiality in Mediation: The Need for Protection" (1986) 2 *Ohio State Journal on Dispute Resolution* 37; ML Prigoff, "Toward Candor or Chaos: The Case of Confidentiality in Mediation" (1988) *Seton Hall Legislative Journal* 1, 103.

5. Lon L Fuller, "Mediation — Its Forms and Functions" (1971) 44 *Southern California Law Review* 305 at 308.

6. Owen V Gray, "Protecting the Confidentiality of Communications in Mediation" (1998) 36(4) *Osgoode Hall Law Journal* 667 ("*Gray*") at 671.

7. Joshua P Rosenburg, "Keeping the Lid on Confidentiality: Mediation Privilege and Conflicts of Laws" (1994) 10(1) *Ohio State Journal on Dispute Resolution* 157 at 161.

8. "Protecting Confidentiality in Mediation" (1984) 98(2) *Harvard Law Review* 441 at 445.

9. Ibid at 441.

10. *Pardy & Pou*, see above note 1 at 55 citing Ellen E Deason, "The Need for Trust as a Justification for Confidentiality in Mediation: A Cross-Disciplinary Approach" (2006) 54 *University of Kansas Law Review* 1387.

11. See above note 8 at 441.

12. Nadja Alexander, *International and Comparative Mediation: Legal Perspectives* (Kluwer Law International 2009) ("*Alexander*") at 246.

13. Ibid.

14. *Gray*, see above note 6 at 671.

15. John P McCrory, "Environmental Mediation — Another Piece for the Puzzle" (1981) 6 *Vermont Law Review* 49 at 56; JB Stulberg, "The Theory and Practice of Mediation: A Reply to Professor Susskind" (1981) 6 *Vermont Law Review* 85 at 87, 95–96.

16. See PJ Harter, "Neither Cop Nor Collection Agent: Encouraging Administrative Settlements by Ensuring Mediator Confidentiality" (1989) 41 *Administrative Law Review* 315 at 325.

17. See above note 8 at 446.

18. Pardy & Pou, see above note 1 at 55, citing Deason, see above note 10 at 1387.

19. Edward J Imwinkelried, "The New Wigmore: An Essay on Rethinking the Foundation of Evidentiary Privileges" (2003) 83 *Boston University Law Review* 315 at 327.

End Notes 147

20. Halsey v Milton Keynes General NHS Trust and Steel v Joy and Halliday [2004] 4 All England Law Reports 920, cited in *Alexander*, see above note 12 at 246.

21. Stephen B Goldberg, Frank EA Sander & Nancy H Rogers, *Dispute Resolution: Negotiation, Mediation and Other Processes*, (Aspen Law & Business, 2nd Edition, 1992) at 179.

22. David Spencer & Michael Brogan, *Mediation Law and Practice* (Melbourne: Cambridge University Press, 2007) (*"Spencer & Brogan"*) at 314.

23. *Spencer & Brogan*, see above note 22 at 468.

24. *Gray*, see above note 6 at 689.

25. J Brad Reich, "A Call for Intellectual Honesty: A Response to the Uniform Mediation Act's Privilege Against Disclosure" (2001) *Journal of Dispute Resolution* 197 at 209, cited in *Alexander*, see above note 12 at 246; Kenneth S Broun, "Giving Codification a Second Chance — Testimonial Privileges and the Federal Rules of Evidence" (2002) 53 *Hastings Law Journal* 769 at 793; Scott H Hughes, "A Closer Look: The Case for a Mediation Confidentiality Privilege Has Not Been Made" (1999) 12:1 *Dispute Resolution Magazine* at 14.

26. Ibid.

27. *Alexander*, see above note 12 at 246.

28. Three Rivers DC v Bank of England (No.4) [2004] United Kingdom House of Lords 48; [2005] 1 Appeal Cases 610 at [28]; affirmed in AKC Koo, "Confidentiality of Mediation Communications" (2011) 30(2) *Civil Justice Quarterly* 192 at 197.

29. Ellen E Deason, "The Quest for Uniformity in Mediation Confidentiality: Foolish Consistency or Crucial Predictability?" (2001) 85 *Marquette Law Review* 79 at 83.

30. Maureen A Weston, "Confidentiality's Constitutionality: The Incursion on Judicial Powers to Regulate Party Conduct in Court-Connected Mediation" (2003) 8 *Harvard Negotiation Law Review* 29 (*"Weston"*) at 49.

31. Anne M Burr, "Confidentiality in Mediation Communications: A Privilege Worth Protecting" (2002) 57:1 *Dispute Resolution Journal* 64.

32. *Spencer & Brogan*, see above note 22 at 313.

33. [2009] Building Law Reports 399 at [44].

34. See above note 8 at 441.

35. See Unilever plc v The Procter & Gamble Co [2001] 1 All England Law Reports 783 at 791–793 where the English court recognised eight instances in which the protection conferred by Without Prejudice privilege would be withheld. This decision has been endorsed in Sin Lian Heng Construction

Pte Ltd v Singapore Telecommunications Ltd [2007] 2 Singapore Law Reports 433; [2007] Singapore High Court 22 at [12].

36. Community Mediation Centres Act, Cap 49A (Rev Ed 1998).

37. Evidence Act, Cap 97 (Rev Ed 1997).

38. Ibid. Section 23(1)(b) of the Evidence Act provides that an admission is not relevant if it was made "upon circumstances from which the court can infer that the parties agreed" that evidence of it would not be given".

39. Ibid.

40. Section 2 of the Mediation Act includes anything said or done, document prepared, or information provided for the purpose of the mediation.

41. Section 9(2)(a) of the Mediation Act.

42. Note that it has been argued that allowing disclosure against the mediator's wishes disadvantages the mediator; see Dorcas Quek Anderson, "A Coming of Age for Mediation in Singapore? Mediation Act 2016" (2017) 29 *Singapore Academy of Law Journal* 275 ("*Quek*") at 282.

43. Section 9(1) of the Mediation Act.

44. *Quek*, see above note 45 at 276; Quek notes that Section 6(2)(a) effectively excludes mediation programmes run by the Community Mediation Centres, the Tripartite Alliance for Dispute Management under the Ministry of Manpower and the Small Claims Tribunals, while Section 6(2)(b) effectively excludes mediations conducted by judges, staff or volunteers of the Family Justice Courts and the State Courts.

45. Section 9(3) read with Section 11(1) of the Mediation Act.

46. Section 10 read with Section 11(1) of the Mediation Act.

47. Sections 11(3) and 11(4) of the Mediation Act.

48. Section 11(2)(b) and (c) states that the court or tribunal must, in deciding whether to grant leave, take into account the public interests of the "administration of justice" and "any circumstances…that the court… considers relevant".

49. *Gray*, see above note 6 at 702.

50. *Weston*, see above note 30.

51. The Uniform Mediation Act (2003) was enacted to address the core concern of the confidentiality of mediation proceedings. It is intended as a statute of general applicability that will apply to almost all mediations. See https://www.mediate.com/articles/umafinalstyled.cfm for more information.

52. *Alexander*, see above note 12 at 246.

53. Section 6(a) of the UMA provides that there is no privilege for mediation communication in 7 instances: (1) in an agreement evidenced by a record signed by all parties to the agreement; (2) available to the public under a

statute or law; (3) a threat or statement of a plan to inflict bodily injury or commit a crime of violence; (4) intentionally used to plan a crime, attempt to commit or commit a crime, or to conceal an ongoing crime or ongoing criminal activity; (5) sought or offered to prove or disprove a claim or complaint of professional misconduct or malpractice filed against a mediator; (6) sought or offered to prove or disprove a claim or complaint of professional misconduct or malpractice filed against a mediation party, nonparty participant, or representative of a party based on conduct occurring during a mediation; and (7) sought or offered to prove or disprove abuse, neglect, abandonment, or exploitation in a proceeding in which a child or adult protective services agency is a party.

54. Section 6(b) of the UMA gives the court or tribunal discretion to circumvent confidentiality if the court or tribunal finds that need for the evidence outweighs the interest in protecting confidentiality.

55. Section 6(b) of the UMA allows disclosure where the communication sought to be disclosed in a court proceeding involves a felony or misdemeanour, or is required for the enforcement of a contract arising out of mediation. The provision also provides for in-camera hearings before a judge for a party to present his/her case so that the court would be able to determine whether the circumvention of confidentiality is justified.

56. Section 6(d) of the UMA.

57. Parliamentary Debates: Official Report, Vol 94 (10 January 2017) (Senior Minister of State for Law: Indranee Rajah S.C.).

Chapter 7 A Review of Mediator Neutrality

1. In Singapore, Codes of Conduct for mediators all require for mediators to be neutral, independent and/or impartial. Examples include the Singapore International Mediation Institute (SIMI) Code of Professional Conduct (2017), Singapore Mediation Centre (SMC) Code of Conduct for Adjudicators (2017) and the Law Society of Singapore's Mediation Scheme Handbook (2017).

2. Ellen Waldman & Lola Akin Ojelabi, "Mediators and Substantive Justice: A View from Rawl's Original Position" (2016) 30(3) *Ohio State Journal on Dispute Resolution* 291 ("*Waldman & Ojelabi*") at 400–404.

3. Susan Douglas, "Neutrality in Mediation: A Study of Mediator Perceptions" (2008) 8(1) *QUT Law and Justice Journal* 139 ("*Douglas*") at 150.

4. This can be further separated into external or internal forms of bias, both of which require different methods of training to combat. See generally Carol

Izumi, "Implicit Bias and the Illusion of Mediator Neutrality" (2010) 34 *Washington University Journal of Law and Policy* 71 ("*Izumi*") at 123–153.

5. *Douglas*, see above note 3.
6. *Douglas*, see above note 3 at 144–145.
7. *Izumi*, see above note 4 at 76.
8. *Douglas*, see above note 3.
9. *Douglas*, see above note 3 at 145–147.
10. *Douglas*, see above note 3 at 147–148.
11. *Waldman & Ojelabi*, see above note 2 at 407 as well as Joseph B. Stulberg, "Must a Mediator be Neutral? You'd Better Believe It!" (2012) 95 *Marquette Law Review* 829 ("*Stulberg*") at 857–858.
12. *Douglas*, see above note 3 at 147.
13. *Douglas*, see above note 3 at 146.
14. *Douglas*, see above note 3 at 148–149.
15. *Izumi*, see above note 4 at 76.
16. Mary Anne Noone & Lola Akin Ojelabi, "Ethical Challenges for Mediators around the Globe: An Australian Perspective" (2014) 45 *Washington University Journal of Law and Policy* 145 ("*Noone & Ojelabi*") at 183.
17. *Noone & Ojelabi*, see above note 16 at 187–189.
18. *Noone & Ojelabi*, see above note 16 at 187–189.
19. *Stulberg*, see above note 11 at 854–856.
20. *Stulberg*, see above note 11 at 857.
21. For example, the Code of Conduct for Adjudicators from the Singapore Mediation Centre (1 April 2017) Rule 2.1 require for adjudicators to maintain the integrity and fairness of the process. The Law Society of Singapore's Mediation Scheme Handbook (2017), Part 6 Clause 11 also requires mediators to respect the parties' right to decide and to assist them in coming to their decision (which must still solely be theirs).
22. *Izumi*, see above note 4 at 83.
23. *Waldman & Ojelabi*, see above note 2 at 407 and *Stulberg*, see above note 11 at 857–858.
24. *Noone & Ojelabi*, see above note 16 at 155.
25. Law Society of Singapore, Mediation Scheme Handbook (2017), Part 6 Clause 15.
26. Family Justice Courts Singapore Website, Mediation/Counselling <https://www.familyjusticecourts.gov.sg/Common/Pages/MediationCounselling.aspx> (accessed 19 February 2018). This is also the stance in Australia: Donna Cooper and Rachael Field, "The Family Dispute Resolution of

Parenting Matters in Australia: An Analysis of the Notion of An 'Independent' Practitioner" (2008) 8(1) *QUT Law and Justice Journal* 158 at 161.

27. Mediation Act 2017, No. 1 of 2017, Section 12(4).
28. *Waldman & Ojelabi*, see above note 2 at 422.
29. National Mediator Accreditation Standards (NMAS) Practice Standards, 1 July 2015, Clause 5.
30. *Noone & Ojelabi*, see above note 16 at 189.
31. For example, the Law Society of Singapore gives certain substantive grounds on which mediation may be terminated by the mediator but the codes of conduct from the SIMI and SMC do not mention such grounds.
32. *Izumi*, see above note 4.
33. *Noone & Ojelabi*, see above note 16 at 184–186.

Chapter 8 The Ethical Boundaries of Honesty in Mediation

1. There are, of course, clearly morally acceptable ways of using this information. For example, you could concede the care and control issue upfront, and try to use the goodwill generated for the division of matrimonial assets.
2. From the perspective of the client and the mediation advocate, it would be a rather callous party indeed who would use a child as a bargaining chip, even in pretense.
3. To be clear, this is purely an intellectual exercise on the ethical boundaries of mediation. I am not advocating lying as a mediation tactic.
4. See Menkel Meadow, "Toward Another View of Legal Negotiation: The Structure of Problem Solving" (1983–1984) 31 *UCLA Law Review* 754.
5. See Russell Korobkin, "Against Integrative Bargaining"(2008) 58 *Case Western Reserve Law Review* 1323.
6. This may be contrasted with a consequentialist approach, like utilitarianism.
7. See, for example, Section 8A(3) of the Legal Profession (Professional Conduct) Rules 2015: 'A legal practitioner must act in good faith throughout the alternative dispute resolution process.'
8. HSBC Institutional Trust Services (Singapore) Ltd (Trustee of Starhill Global Real Estate Investment Trust) v Toshin Development Singapore Pte Ltd [2012] Singapore Court of Appeal 48; [2012] 4 Singapore Law Reports 738.
9. Auld LJ in Street v Derbyshire Unemployed Workers' Centre [2004] 4 All England Law Reports 839 at [41].
10. United Group Rail Services Ltd v Rail Corporation NSW [2009] New South Wales Court of Appeal 177.

152 *Contemporary Issues in Mediation Volume 4*

11. From a strictly legal position and as a matter of self-interest, the mediation advocate should obviously follow his legal duty of good faith and not do anything illegal. But we are concerned with the ethical position here.

12. Hooper Bailie Associated Ltd v Natcon Group Pty Ltd [1992] 28 New South Wales Court of Appeal 194.

13. See Avnita Lakhani (2007) "The Truth About Lying as a Negotiation Tactic: Where Business, Ethics, and Law Collide … Or Do They?," 9(6) *ADR Bulletin* Article 2.

14. See Roger Fisher, William Ury & Bruce Patton, *Getting to Yes: Negotiating Agreement Without Giving In* (Winnipeg: Media Production Services Unit, 2013).

15. See the holding of Evans J in Wales v Wadham [1977] 1 Weekly Law Reports 199: "A statement of intention is not a representation of existing fact, unless the person making it does not honestly hold the intention he is expressing, in which case there is a misrepresentation of fact in relation to the state of that person's mind." Cited with approval in Tan Chin Seng and others v Raffles Town Club Pte Ltd [2003] 3 Singapore Law Reports (Reissue) 307.

16. See Dimmock v Hallet [1866] 2 Law Reports Chancery Appeals 21: A half-truth or suppression of material facts can constitute a misrepresentation if it omits material facts.

Chapter 9 Negotiating with Children and How that Teaches Us to Be Better Mediators

1. For example, see recent commentary in Channel NewsAsia where the author encourages negotiation as a parenting style to prevent excessively giving in to children: Foo Koong Hean, "Smaller Families in Singapore, leading to unhealthy parenting style", *Channel NewsAsia* (27 August 2017) <http://www.channelnewsasia.com/news/singapore/commentary-smaller-families-in-singapore-leading-to-unhealthy-9112070> (accessed 15 March 2018).

2. Roger Fisher, William Ury & Bruce Patton, *Getting to Yes: Negotiating an Agreement Without Giving In* (New York: Penguin Group, 2nd Edition, 1991) ("*Getting to Yes*") at 6.

3. Ibid.

4. Malin Alfven & Kristina Hofsten, *Time out! A Parent's Guide to Understanding and Dealing with Challenging Children*, (New York: Skyhorse Publishing, 2015) ("*Alfven & Hofsten*") at 43.

5. *Getting to Yes*, see above note 2 at 35.

6. *Getting to Yes*, see above note 2 at 25.

7. William Ury, *Getting Past No: Negotiating in Difficult Situations*, reissue (New York: Bantam Dell, 2007) ("*Getting Past No*") at 81.

8. Robert Mayer, *How to Win Any Negotiation Without Raising Your Voice, Losing Your Cool or Coming to Blows* (New York: Career Press, 2006) at 63. For example, "I was wondering what you thought of my proposal."

9. This account is also reinforced by a personal interview with a department head at a special school in Singapore for high-functioning children with autism.

10. *Getting Past No*, see above note 7 at 82.

11. Kim Abraham & Marney Studaker-Cordner, "Negotiating with Kids: When You Should and Shouldn't", Empowering Parents.com <https://www.empoweringparents.com/article/negotiating-with-kids-when-you-should-and-shouldnt/> (accessed 10 March 2018) ("*Abraham & Cordner*").

12. "10 Hard-Bargaining Tactics and Negotiation Skills: The best hard-bargaining tactics that can catch you off guard", Programme on Negotiation, Harvard Law School (18 February 2018) <https://www.pon.harvard.edu/daily/batna/10-hardball-tactics-in-negotiation/> (accessed 10 March 2018).

13. *Abraham & Cordner*, see above note 11.

14. *Getting Past No*, see above note 7 at 49.

15. "Negotiating Lessons Learned from Kids with Steve Young", interview by Stanford University, ECorner (22 May 2007) <http://ecorner.stanford.edu/videos/1773/Negotiation-Lessons-Learned-from-Kids> (accessed 20 March 2018) ("*Steve Young*"). Steve Young was a former National Football League Quarterback and was named the NFL's Most Valuable Player in 1992 and 1994, and was the MVP of Super Bowl XXIX.

16. *Steve Young*, see above note 15.

17. Ibid.

18. Jeff Weiss, *HBR Guide to Negotiating* (Boston: Harvard Business School Publishing, 2016) ("*Weiss*") at 86.

19. *Alfven & Hofsten*, see above note 4 at 86.

20. *Weiss*, see above note 18 at 87.

21. *Getting to Yes*, see above note 2 at 20.

22. Roger Fisher & Scott Brown, *Getting Together: Building Relationships As We Negotiate* (New York: Penguin Books, 1989) ("*Fisher & Brown*") at 97.

23. *Alfven & Hofsten*, see above note 4 at 94.

24. *Getting Past No*, see above note 7 at 59.

25. *Getting Past No*, see above note 7 at 61.

26. *Fisher & Brown*, see above note 22 at 59.

27. Jennifer Gerarda Brown, "The Role of Apology in Negotiation" (2003) 87 *Marquette Law Review* 665 (2003) at 669.

28. *Getting Past No*, see above note 7 at 32.
29. *Getting Past No*, see above note 7 at 31. Ambrose Bierce (24 June 1982–1914) was an American Civil War soldier and writer.
30. Anna Maxted, "No more negotiating, I've learned to say NO to my children", *DailyMail* (9 May 2012) <http://www.dailymail.co.uk/femail/article-2142115/No-negotiating-Ive-learned-say-NO-children.html> (accessed 18 March 2018).
31. *Fisher & Brown*, see above note 22 at 53.
32. Getting Past No, see above note 7 at 48.
33. Niveen Iskandar, Brett Laursen, Benjamin Finkelstein & Laen Fredrickson, "Conflict Resolution Among Preschool Children: The Appeal of Negotiation in Hypothetical Disputes" (1995) 6(4), *Early Education and Development* 359 ("*Iskandar et al.*") at 364. Note: study was conducted on 48 children enrolled in 5 half-day university laboratory nursery school classes. For more details, refer to page 361 for methodology in the study.
34. *Iskandar et al.*, see above note 33 at 368.
35. *Iskandar et al.*, see above note 33 at 368: "Younger pre-schoolers may recognise a mature form of conflict resolution in a hypothetical situation, yet not have the skills to recall or enact the same sophisticated strategy in daily disputes."
36. *Alfven & Hofsten*, see above note 4 at 75.
37. For an example, refer to "Barbie Dolphin Magic Transforming Mermaid Doll" <https://www.amazon.com/Barbie-Dolphin-Magic-Transforming-Mermaid/dp/B01N5HMSCH/ref=sr_1_3_sspa?s=toys-and-games&ie=UTF8&qid=1509703234&sr=1-3-spons&keywords=barbie+doll&psc=1> (accessed 20 March 2018).
38. *Getting to Yes*, see above note 2 at 32.
39. *Getting to Yes*, see above note 2 at 32.
40. Bill Adler JR, *How to Negotiate like a Child: Unleash the Little Monster Within to Get Everything You Want* (New York: AMACOM, 2006) ("*Adler*") at 148.
41. *Adler*, see above note 40 at 65.
42. *Getting to Yes*, see above note 2 at 28.
43. *Fisher & Brown*, see above note 22 at 11.
44. *Adler*, see above note 40 at 121.
45. *Adler*, see above note 40 at 122.
46. *Getting to Yes*, see above note 2 at 39.
47. *Weiss*, see above note 18 at 168.

Chapter 10 Learning from Crises: How Crisis Negotiation Skills Can Help Mediators Deal with Parties in Mediation

1. Andy Raskin, "To Be a Better Leader, Learn This FBI Hostage Negotiation Tactic", *The Mission* (27 July 2016) <https://medium.com/the-mission/this-fbi-hostage-negotiation-tactic-makes-you-a-better-leader-a4afe919c18d> (accessed 7 March 2018).
2. Carole J. Brown, "Facilitative Mediation: The Classic Approach Retains Its Appeal", Mediate.com (December 2002) <https://www.mediate.com/articles/brownc.cfm> (accessed 7 March 2018).
3. Julie Denny, "The Importance of Emotions in Mediation", Mediate.com (June 2013) <https://www.mediate.com/articles/DennyJ2.cfm> (accessed 7 March 2018).
4. Senyo M. Adjabeng, "Mediation and the Principle of Neutrality", Mediate. com (April 2006) <https://www.mediate.com/articles/adjabengS1. cfm?nl=101> (accessed 30 March 2018).
5. Ronald Loh, "Police Crisis Negotiation Unit: Keeping calm when crisis is on", *The New Paper* (30 May 2016) <http://www.tnp.sg/news/singapore/police-crisis-negotiation-unit-keeping-calm-when-crisis> (accessed 7 March 2018).
6. Michael McMains & Wayman Mullins, *Crisis Negotiations: Managing Critical Incidents and Hostage Situations in Law Enforcement and Corrections* (Routledge, 5th Edition, 2014) ("*McMains & Mullins*") at 247.
7. Jeff Thompson, "Crisis Hostage Negotiation and the Impact of 'Control'", *Psychology Today* (19 September 2017) <https://www.psychologytoday. com/us/blog/beyond-words/201709/crisis-hostage-negotiation-and-the-impact-control> (accessed 7 March 2018).
8. Chris Voss & Tahl Raz, *Never Split the Difference: Negotiating As If Your Life Depended On It* (Random House, 2016) ("*Voss & Tahl*") at 17.
9. Roger Fisher, William Ury & Bruce Patton, *Getting to Yes: Negotiating Agreement Without Giving In* (New York: Penguin Group, 2nd Edition, 1991) at 13 and 19.
10. Keld Jensen, "Why Negotiators Still Aren't 'Getting to Yes", *Forbes* (5 February 2013) <https://www.forbes.com/sites/keldjensen/2013/02/05/why-negotiators-still-arent-getting-to-yes/#1601e0a12640> (accessed 7 March 2018).
11. *Voss & Tahl*, see above note 8 at 17–18.
12. Kimberlyn Leary, Julianna Pillemer & Michael Wheeler, "Negotiating with Emotion", *Harvard Business Review* (January–February 2013)

<https://hbr.org/2013/01/negotiating-with-emotion> (accessed 7 March 2018) ("*Leary et al.*").

13. *Voss & Tahl*, see above note 8 at 23.
14. *McMains & Mullins*, see above note 6 at 163.
15. Tony Bogdanoski, "The Importance and Challenge of Active Listening in Mediation", *Australasian Dispute Resolution Journal* 20(4) (2009) at 207–209.
16. *Voss & Tahl*, see above note 8) at 19.
17. *Voss & Tahl*, see above note 8) at 35.
18. Leary *et al.*, see above note 12.
19. Jeff Thompson, "The 5 Core Skills Of Hostage Negotiators", *Psychology Today* (5 October 2015) <https://www.psychologytoday.com/us/blog/beyond-words/201510/the-5-core-skills-hostage-negotiators> (accessed 11 March 2018).
20. *McMains & Mullins*, see above note 6 at 128.
21. Eric Barker, "6 Hostage Negotiation Techniques That Will Get You What You Want", *TIME* (26 March 2014) <http://time.com/38796/6-hostage-negotiation-techniques-that-will-get-you-what-you-want> (accessed 7 March 2018) ("*Barker*").
22. Ibid.
23. *McMains & Mullins*, see above note 6 at 129.
24. Ibid.
25. *Voss & Tahl*, see above note 8 at 103.
26. *McMains & Mullins*, see above note 6 at 129.
27. Ibid.
28. *Voss & Tahl*, see above note 8 at 40.
29. Ibid.
30. Ibid.
31. *McMains & Mullins*, see above note 6 at 130.
32. *Voss & Tahl*, see above note 8 at 56.
33. *Barker*, see above note 21.
34. *Voss & Tahl*, see above note 8 at 59.
35. *Voss & Tahl*, see above note 8 at 59–60.
36. *Voss & Tahl*, see above note 8 at 58.
37. *Barker*, see above note 21.
38. Karyn Hall, "Understanding Validation: A Way To Communicate Acceptance", *Psychology Today* (26 April 2012) <https://www.psychologytoday.com/us/blog/pieces-mind/201204/understanding-validation-way-communicate-acceptance> (accessed 9 March 2018).

End Notes 157

39. *Voss & Tahl*, see above note 8 at 58 and 65.
40. *Voss & Tahl*, see above note 8 at 60.
41. *Voss & Tahl*, see above note 8 at 62–63.
42. *Voss & Tahl*, see above note 8 at 56.
43. Jeff Thompson, "Active Listening Techniques of Hostage & Crisis Negotiators", *Psychology Today* (5 November 2013) <https://www.psychologytoday.com/us/blog/beyond-words/201311/active-listening-techniques-hostage-crisis-negotiators> (accessed 7 March 2018).
44. *Voss & Tahl*, see above note 8 at 99.
45. Andy Raskin, "To Be a Better Leader, Learn This FBI Hostage Negotiation Tactic", *The Mission* (27 July 2016) <https://medium.com/the-mission/this-fbi-hostage-negotiation-tactic-makes-you-a-better-leader-a4afe919c18d> (accessed 7 March 2018).
46. *Voss & Tahl*, see above note 8) at 112.
47. *Voss & Tahl*, see above note 8 at 112.
48. *Voss & Tahl*, see above note 8 at 103–104.
49. *McMains & Mullins*, see above note 6 at 178.
50. *McMains & Mullins*, see above note 6 at 176.
51. *McMains & Mullins*, see above note 6 at 175.
52. *McMains & Mullins*, see above note 6 at 176.
53. Ibid.
54. *Voss & Tahl*, see above note 8 at 140.
55. *Voss & Tahl*, see above note 8 at 153.
56. *Voss & Tahl*, see above note 8 at 153.
57. *Voss & Tahl*, see above note 8 at 208–210. Griffin's only interest was in getting the police to kill him — he wanted to die, and his hostages were not needed alive for that.
58. H.A. Hellyer, "Why Isis Cannot Be Negotiated With", *The Atlantic* (10 January 2016) <https://www.theatlantic.com/international/archive/2016/01/what-to-do-about-isis negotiations/423432> (accessed 21 March 2018).
59. "Issue 9 of ISIS' 'Rumiyah' Magazine Promotes New Angle To Taking Westerners Hostages — Solely for Execution and Giving ISIS Publicity", MEMRI (5 May 2017) <https://www.memri.org/jttm/issue-9-isiss-rumiyah-magazine-promotes-new-angle-%E2%80%8E-taking-westerners-hostages-%E2%80%93-solely> (accessed 21 March 2018).
60. *Voss & Tahl*, see above note 8 at 212–213.

Chapter 11 Equal but Different? Exploring How Gender Roles Shape the Power Balance in Family-Related Mediation

1. Jordi Agustí-Panareda, "Power Imbalances in Mediation: Questioning Some Common Assumptions" (2004) 59 *Dispute Resolution Journal* 24 ("*Agustí-Panareda*") at 26.
2. Joan B. Kelly, "Power Imbalance in Divorce and Interpersonal Mediation: Assessment and Intervention" (1995) 13 *Conflict Resolution Quarterly* 85 ("*Kelly*") at 87.
3. James B. Boskey, "Negotiation Journal: On the Process of Dispute Settlement" (1994) 10 *Negotiation Journal* 308 ("*Boskey*").
4. *Kelly*, see above note 2 at 87.
5. *Agustí-Panareda*, see above note 1 at 26.
6. Astor Hilary, "Violence and Family Mediation Policy" (1994) 8 *Australian Journal of Family Law* 3 ("*Hilary*").
7. Astor Hilary, *Guidelines for Use if Mediating in Cases Involving Violence Against Women* (National Committee on Violence Against Women, 1992).
8. Rachel M. Field, "Mediation and the Art of Power (Im)Balancing" (1998) 12 *QUT Law Journal* 271 ("*Field*").
9. *Kelly*, see above note 2 at 87.
10. Ann Williams, "No improvement in Singapore's gender pay gap since 2006: Report", *The Straits Time* (17 August 2017) <http://www.straitstimes.com/business/economy/no-improvement-in-singapores-gender-pay-gap-since-2006-report> (accessed 8 April 2018).
11. Kathy Mack, "Alternative Dispute Resolution and Access to Justice for Women" (1995) 17 *Adelaide Law Review* 123 ("*Mack*") at 124.
12. *Hilary*, see above note 6 at 5.
13. Ibid.
14. LG Lerman, "Stopping Domestic Violence: A Guide for Mediators" in H Davidson, L Ray & R Horowitz, eds., *Alternative Means of Family Dispute Resolution* (Washington DC: American Bar Association, 1982), 429–443.
15. *Mack*, see above note 11 at 124.
16. Certain features that are associated with powerlessness are more frequently used by women (such as the use of superlative/filler words, voices that tend to be higher-pitched in general and so forth).
17. Christopher W. Moore, *The Mediation Process: Practical Strategies for Resolving Conflict* (San Francisco: Jossey-Bass, 2003).
18. Dafna Lavi, "Till Death Do Us Part: Online Mediation as an Answer to Divorce Cases Involving Violence" (2015) 16(2) *North Carolina Journal of Law & Technology* 264 ("*Lavi*").

End Notes 159

19. *Lavi*, see above note 18 at 264.
20. Albie Davis & Richard Salem, "Dealing with Power Imbalances in the Mediation of Interpersonal Disputes" (1984) 6 *Mediation Quarterly* 17 (*"Davis & Salem"*) at 18.
21. Lydia Belzer, "Domestic Abuse and Divorce Mediation: Suggestions for a Safer Process" (2004) 5 *Loyola Journal of Public Interest Law* at 49–50 (*"Belzer"*).
22. *Lavi*, see above note 18 at 267–273.
23. *Boskey*, see above note 3 at 308.
24. Stella Tarrant, "Something Is Pushing Them To the Side of Their Own Lives: A Feminist Critique of Law and Laws" (1990) 20 *Western Australian Law Review* 573 at 581.
25. *Mack*, see above note 11 at 124.
26. Martha Bailey, "Unpacking the "Rational Alternative": A Critical Review of Family Mediation Movement Claims" (1989) *Canadian Journal of Family Law* 61 (*"Bailey"*) at 69.
27. Emeritus Professor of Flinders University.
28. *Bailey*, see above note 26 at 69.
29. *Mack*, see above note 11 at 124.
30. Chief Justice Sundaresh Menon, "Role of Courts Regarding Recent Family Issues — How To Tackle Family Issues On Child Welfare And Domestic Violence", at para [18], 17th Conference of Chief Justices of Asia And The Pacific in Tokyo, Japan (19–21 September 2017). <https://www.supremecourt.gov.sg/Data/Editor/Documents/cj-39-s-paper-for-17th-conference-of-chief-justices-of-asia-and-the-pacific.pdf> (accessed 26 April 2018).
31. *Lavi*, see above note 18 277–278.
32. *Davis & Salem*, see above note 20 at 18.
33. *Bailey*, see above note 26 at 69.
34. *Lavi*, see above note 18 at 277–278.
35. *Belzer*, see above note 21.
36. *Field*, see above note 7 at 272.
37. Aimee Davis, "Mediating Cases Involving Domestic Violence: Solution of Setback?" (2007) 8 *Cardozo Journal of Conflict Resolution* 253 at 268.
38. *Davis & Salem*, see above note 20 at 18.
39. Author Unknown, "2018 Women in Mediation: An Interview with Sabiha Shiraz" Singapore International Mediation Institute (28 March 2018) <http://www.simi.org.sg/Resources/Feature/IWHM/2018/SabihaShiraz> (accessed 1 April 2018).
40. Ibid.

160　*Contemporary Issues in Mediation Volume 4*

41. Jeffrey Rubin & William Zartman, "Asymmetrical Negotiations: Some Survey Results that may Surprise" (1995) 11(4) *Negotiation Journal* 349 ("*Rubin & Zartman*") at 350.
42. *Agustí-Panareda*, see above note 1 at 26.
43. *Rubin & Zartman*, see above note 41 at 350.
44. *Agustí-Panareda*, see above note 1 at 27.
45. Ibid.
46. BC Bedont, "Gender Differences in Negotiations and the Doctrine of Unconscionability in Domestic Contracts" (1994) 12 *Canadian Family Law Quarterly* 21 at 34.
47. SL Borys, "The Relation of Power, Goals, and Gender to Preferences for Various Conflict Resolution Settings" (1987) (Unpublished thesis, University of Waterloo).
48. JH Wade, "Forms of Power in Family Mediation and Negotiation" (1994) 8 *Australian Journal of Family Law* 40.
49. Joel Lee & Teh Hwee Hwee, *Asian Culture: A Definitional Challenge* (Singapore: Academy Publishing, 2009) at 54–61.
50. Charlene Tan, "Our Shared Values in Singapore: A Confucian Perspective" (2012) 62(4) *Educational Theory* 449.
51. John Barkai, "What's a Cross Cultural Mediator to Do? A Low-Context Solution for a High-Context Problem" (2008) 10 *Cardozo Journal of Conflict Resolution* 43 at 82.
52. Irene K.H. Chew & Christopher Lim, "A Confucian perspective on conflict resolution" (1995) *The International Journal of Human Resource Management* 143 at 145.
53. Kenneth Ian Macduff, "Decision-making and Commitments: Impact of Power Distance in Mediation" in Joel Lee & Teh Hwee Hwee, eds., *An Asian Perspective on Mediation* (Singapore: Academy Publishing, 2009) at 124.
54. *Kelly*, see above note 2 at 87.
55. *Lavi*, see above note 18 at 277–278.
56. Women's Charter, Cap 353 (Rev Ed 2009), Section 50(3A).

Chapter 12　Are All Expressions of Anger Equal or Are Some More Equal Than Others?

1. Roger Fisher & William Ury, *Getting to Yes: Negotiating Agreement Without Giving In* (New York: Penguin Books, 1991).

2. Jessica Katz Jameson, Andrea M. Bodtker & Tricia S. Jones, "Like Talking to a Brick Wall: Implications of Emotion Metaphors for Mediation Practice" (2006) 22(2) *Negotiation Journal* 199 ("*Jameson et al.*").

3. Jessica Katz Jameson, Andrea M. Bodtker & Tim Linker, "Facilitating Conflict Transformation: Mediator Strategies for Eliciting Emotional Communication in a Workplace Conflict" (2010) 26(1) *Negotiation Journal* 25.

4. Donald E. Gibson & Ronda Roberts Callister, "Anger in Organizations: Review and Integration" (2010) 36(1) Journal of Management 66 at 68.

5. Leigh Thompson, Victoria Husted Medvec, Vanessa Seiden & Shirli Kopelman, "Poker Face, Smiley Face, and Rant 'n' Rave: Myths and Realities About Emotion in Negotiation" in Michael A. Hogg & R. Scott Tindale, eds., *Blackwell Handbook of Social Psychology: Group Processes* (US: Blackwell Publishers, 2001) at 139–163.

6. Ray Friedman, Cameron Anderson, Jeanne M. Brett, Mara Olekalns, Nathan Goates & Cara Cherry Lisco, "The Positive and Negative Effects of Anger on Dispute Resolution: Evidence from Electronically Mediated Disputes" (2004) 89(2) *Journal of Applied Psychology* 369.

7. Joseph P. Daly, "The Effects of Anger on Negotiations Over Mergers and Acquisitions" (1991) 7(1) *Negotiation Journal* 31.

8. Robert A. Creo, "Embracing and Using Anger in Mediation" (2016) 34(11) *Alternatives to the High Cost of Litigation* 166 ("*Creo*"). See also Tsai Ming-Hong & Maia J. Young, "Anger, Fear, and Escalation of Commitment" (2010) 24(6) *Cognition and Emotion* 962.

9. *Creo*, see above note 8 at 167.

10. Jennifer R. Overbeck, Margaret A. Neale & Cassandra L. Govan, "I Feel, Therefore You Act: Intrapersonal and Interpersonal Effects of Emotion on Negotiation as a Function of Social Power" (2010) 112(2) *Organizational Behavior & Human Decision Processes* 126 ("*Overbeck et al.*").

11. *Overbeck et al.*, see above note 10.

12. Cheryl Picard & Janet Siltanen, "Exploring the Significance of Emotion for Mediation Practice" (2013) 31(1) *Conflict Resolution Quarterly* 31.

13. *Jameson et al.*, see above note 2.

14. Gerben A. Van Kleef, Carsten K. W. De Dreu, Davide Pietroni & Antony S. R. Manstead, "Power and Emotion in Negotiation: Power Moderates the Interpersonal Effects of Anger and Happiness on Concession Making" (2006) 36(4) *European Journal of Social Psychology* 557 ("*Van Kleef et al.*").

15. *Van Kleef et al.*, see above note 14.

16. Ibid.
17. Gerben A. Van Kleef, Carsten K. W. De Dreu & Antony S. R. Manstead, "The Interpersonal Effects of Anger and Happiness in Negotiations" (2004) 86(1) *Journal of Personality & Social Psychology* 57 (*"Gerben et al."*).
18. *Gerben et al.*, see above note 17.
19. Ibid.
20. Marwan Sinaceur & Larissa Z. Tiedens, "Get Mad and Get More Than Even: When and Why Anger Expression is Effective in Negotiations" (2006) 42(3) *Journal of Experimental Social Psychology* 314.
21. *Gerben et al.*, see above note 17.
22. Ilja Van Beest, Gerben A. Van Kleef & Eric Van Dijk, "Get Angry, Get Out: The Interpersonal Effects of Anger Communication in Multiparty Negotiation" (2008) 44(4) *Journal of Experimental Social Psychology* 993 (*"Van Beest et al."*).
23. *Van Beest et al.*, see above note 22.
24. See for example, Jeswald W. Salacuse, "Ten Ways that Culture Affects Negotiating Style: Some Survey Results" (1998) 14(3) *Negotiation Journal* 221.
25. Hajo Adam, Aiwa Shirako & William W. Maddux, "Cultural Variance in the Interpersonal Effects of Anger in Negotiations" (2010) 21(6) *Psychological Science* 882 (*"Adam et al."*).
26. Shirli Kopelman & Ashleigh Shelby Rosette, "Cultural Variation in Response to Strategic Emotions in Negotiations" (2008) 17(1) *Group Decision and Negotiation* 65 (*"Kopelman & Rosette"*).
27. *Kopelman & Rosette*, see above note 26.
28. Michele J. Gelfand, Marianne Higgins, Lisa H. Nishii, Jana L. Raver, Alexandria Dominguez, Fumio Murakami & Susumu Yamaguchi, "Culture and Egocentric Biases of Fairness in Conflict and Negotiation" (2002) 87(5) *Journal of Applied Psychology* 833.
29. Liu Meina, "The Intrapersonal and Interpersonal Effects of Anger on Negotiation Strategies: A Cross-Cultural Investigation" (2009) 35(1) *Human Communication Research* 148.
30. *Adam et al.*, see above note 25.
31. Gerben A. Van Kleef & Carsten K. W. De Dreu, "Longer-term consequences of anger expression in negotiation: Retaliation or spillover?" (2010) 46(5) *Journal of Experimental Social Psychology* 753 (*"Van Kleef & De Dreu"*).
32. *Van Kleef & De Dreu*, see above note 31.
33. Ray Friedman, Cameron Anderson, Jeanne M. Brett, Mara Olekalns, Nathan Goates & Cara Cherry Lisco, "The positive and negative effects of anger on

dispute resolution: Evidence from electronically mediated disputes" (2004) 89(2) *Journal of Applied Psychology* 369.
34. *Van Kleef & De Dreu*, see above note 31.
35. Ibid.
36. Wang Lu, Gregory B. Northcraft & Gerben A. Van Kleef, "Beyond Negotiated Outcomes: The Hidden Costs of Anger Expression in Dyadic Negotiation" (2012) 119(1) *Organizational Behavior and Human Decision Processes* 54 ("*Wang et al.*").
37. *Wang et al.*, see above note 36.
38. Steven G. Mehta, "Negotiating Games — Using Anger in Mediation, A Researched Analysis" (3 June 2009) <https://stevemehta.wordpress.com/2009/06/03/351> (accessed 8 April 2018).
39. Tng Han-Ying & Al K. C. Au, "Strategic Display of Anger and Happiness in Negotiation: The Moderating Role of Perceived Authenticity" (2014) 30(3) *Negotiation Journal* 301.
40. Stéphane Côté, Ivona Hideg & Gerben A. Van Kleef, "The Consequences of Faking Anger in Negotiations" (2013) 49(3) *Journal of Experimental Social Psychology* 453 ("*Côté et al.*").
41. *Côté et al.*, see above note 40.

CPSIA information can be obtained
at www.ICGtesting.com
Printed in the USA
BVHW040047210819
556281BV00006B/54/P